Better Homes and Gardens®

DECORATING YOUR HOME

Library of Congress Catalog Card Number: 85-61271
ISBN: 0-696-02178-1

BETTER HOMES AND GARDENS® BOOKS

Editor: Gerald M. Knox
Art Director: Ernest Shelton
Managing Editor: David A. Kirchner

Associate Art Directors: Linda Ford Vermie,
Neoma Alt West, Randall Yontz
Copy and Production Editors: Marsha Jahns,
Mary Helen Schiltz, Carl Voss, David A. Walsh
Assistant Art Directors: Lynda Haupert, Harijs Priekulis,
Tom Wegner
Senior Graphic Designers: Alisann Dixon, Mike Eagleton,
Lyne Neymeyer
Graphic Designers: Mike Burns, Sally Cooper, Deb Miner,
Stan Sams, Darla Whipple-Frain

Vice President, Editorial Director: Doris Eby
Group Editorial Services Director: Duane L. Gregg

Senior Vice President, General Manager: Fred Stines
Director of Publishing: Robert B. Nelson
Vice President, Retail Marketing: Jamie Martin
Vice President, Direct Marketing: Arthur Heydendael

All About Your House: Decorating Your Home

Project Editor: James A. Hufnagel
Associate Editor: Willa Rosenblatt Speiser
Assistant Editor: Leonore A. Levy
Copy and Production Editor: Mary Helen Schiltz
Building and Remodeling Editor: Joan McCloskey
Furnishings and Design Editor: Shirley Van Zante
Garden Editor: Douglas A. Jimerson
Money Management and Features Editor: Margaret Daly

Associate Art Director: Linda Ford Vermie
Graphic Designer: Mike Eagleton
Electronic Text Processor: Donna Russell

Contributing Editors: Jill Abeloe Mead, Stephen Mead
Contributors: Denise L. Caringer, Pamela Wilson Cullison,
Leonore Levy, Jill Abeloe Mead, Ann Elizabeth Powell,
Willa Rosenblatt Speiser, Marcia Spires, David Walsh

Special thanks to William N. Hopkins, Bill Hopkins, Jr.,
Babs Klein, and Don Wipperman for their valuable
contributions to this book.

INTRODUCTION

Have you ever agonized over selecting a wall color, drapery fabric, or piece of furniture? If so, you're not alone. To many people, decorating a home seems mysterious, even intimidating. The reason may be that with decorating—unlike building, gardening, or even baking a cake—hard-and-fast rules simply don't apply. Instead, a room can look just right, not quite right, or all wrong for a wide variety of reasons.

A few people seem to have a natural aptitude—or "eye"—for putting together successful room schemes. Consciously or not, however, they're applying general design principles that any of us can master. *Decorating Your Home* explains these principles and tells how you can put them to work at your house.

Here you'll learn about decorating styles and how you can create your own; how to plan and execute decorating changes; the importance of backgrounds; tried-and-true decorating techniques; where to find the furnishings you need; and how to fine-tune your decor with art, accessories, and lighting. The more than 100 color photographs found in this book were chosen to not only delight the eye, but also, we hope, to educate it. In short, *Decorating Your Home* is a short course in decorating your home.

If you like what you see, perhaps you'll want to learn about other ways you can improve your house. If so, the **ALL ABOUT YOUR HOUSE** Library can help. Prepared by the editors of *Better Homes and Gardens*, this series of books adds up to the most comprehensive encyclopedia of home decorating, remodeling, planning, gardening, and management we've ever published.

DECORATING YOUR HOME

CONTENTS

CHAPTER 1

BEGINNING QUESTIONS
6

What are your reasons for decorating?
Do you need a total redo or just touches?
What style suits you best?
Would you like to mix and match styles?

Do you have the space to do what you want?
Could good lighting add drama to your rooms?
What can accessories do for a room?
Do you need the help of a design professional?

CHAPTER 2

EXPRESSING YOUR OWN STYLE
22

Welcome-home rooms
Pure and simple
Timeless heritage

Handcrafted appeal
Mixing and matching
Soft and romantic

CHAPTER 3

PLANNING DECORATING CHANGES
46

Analyzing what you have
Getting started
Deciding what to keep and what to change
Backgrounds

Introducing key elements
Bringing in light
Arranging the pieces
Completing the look

CHAPTER 4

BEAUTIFUL BACKGROUNDS
62

Walls
Ceilings

Floors
Windows

CHAPTER 5

TRIED-AND-TRUE TECHNIQUES
76

Renew a room with fabric
Use color courageously
Use a neutral plus one color
Stay with a single color family
Aim for the right room arrangement

Use one fabric for all it's worth
Call attention to structural details
Strip down your decorating
Strive for personal style

CHAPTER 6

FINDING WHAT YOU NEED 94

Department stores, home stores, and specialty shops
Catalog shopping
Antiques shops and auctions

Design collections
Alternative sources
Professional designers and decorators

CHAPTER 7

DECORATING CASE STUDIES 106

Starting from scratch
A new look on a budget
Improving on what you have

Decorating in stages
Conquering space

CHAPTER 8

FINE-TUNING YOUR DECOR 126

Arranging accessories
Displaying artwork

Choosing lighting

CHAPTER 9

SEWING FOR YOUR HOME 138

Curtains and draperies
Shades
Pillows

Table coverings
Children's accessories

CHAPTER 10

WHEN TO STOP 148

Leave some breathing room
Use wall coverings judiciously

Avoid color cacophony
Prune your patterns

WHERE TO GO FOR MORE INFORMATION 156

ACKNOWLEDGMENTS 157

INDEX 158

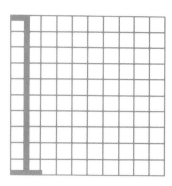

BEGINNING QUESTIONS

If you were to hire a designer to decorate a room or rooms in your home, the designer would most likely take a brief look around, then sit down and ask a series of questions aimed at determining your needs, preferences, priorities, and budget. This introductory chapter asks many of the questions a professional would raise. Answering them for yourself can help you define your decorating problems and goals. Once these are in focus, you can turn to other chapters in the book for solutions.

If you've been giving thought to decorating or redecorating a room or rooms in your home, the first question to ask yourself is why. The answer to this one will help shape your entire course of action.

One big reason people take on a decorating project is that they've just moved in and discovered that the builder's or former owner's taste isn't theirs, or that furnishings that looked great in the last house don't really suit the new one. Similarly, if you move to a house that's larger or smaller than your former home, of a very different architectural style, or in a different region, you may find yourself with furnishings that just don't look right any more, are too large for some rooms, too formal for others, or too summery for winter days.

Another reason for a change might be that your family life has changed. As your children get older, for example, you may begin to feel you'd like more elegant furnishings, fewer child-proof fabrics, and a generally more sophisticated look. Or you may need to make spaces do double-duty to serve an expanding family.

Another possibility, of course, is that you're staying put, but your decorating scheme has seen better days. Colors fade, fabrics wear thin, styles become dated or downright unattractive by current standards. At some point, redecorating becomes not only justified but necessary.

A new look in old space
One more reason for decorating or redecorating could come about if you're making changes in your home's physical layout with an addition or other remodeling project. Then you may need to not only decorate the new space but also adapt the decorating scheme in one or more rooms to suit the new look.

The sunny breakfast corner pictured *opposite* is part of a remodeled kitchen that used to be a service area containing a maid's room, laundry, pantry, back hallway, and small kitchen. It bears little if any resemblance to the family's former eating quarters, which were cramped and dark.

To turn the new space into a sun-porch-style kitchen that worked with the rest of their house, the homeowners had to come up with a unifying scheme. It began with a tongue-and-groove ceiling, characteristic of the era in which the home was built, which contributes its own country flavor to the setting. New French doors and a tile floor further the country look, and also link the new/old space to a patio outside. A simple pine table and matching chairs were carefully chosen to match the new mood created by the architecture.

To visually unite this room with the adjacent kitchen (not shown), the homeowners used the same flooring and ceiling treatments there, along with moldings that have a period flair.

For more about points to consider when you're deciding why, when, and how to redecorate, see Chapter 3—"Planning Decorating Changes"—and Chapter 7—"Decorating Case Studies."

DO YOU NEED A TOTAL REDO OR JUST TOUCHES?

Once you've decided why you want a decorating change, the next step is to figure out just how much to change. If you're basically happy with much of your decor, but feel that it needs a new spark, a relatively limited approach—such as painting the walls, changing a few accessories, or hanging new art work—can have a surprisingly dramatic effect. If, on the other hand, much of a room looks drab or doesn't fit your tastes and life-style, you'll probably want, and need, to go several steps further—on to repainting, repapering, reupholstering key pieces, or purchasing major new items. Here's a case where a series of small changes made a big difference.

The eclectic living room pictured *at right* reflects the evolution of one family's tastes, budget, and life-style. The soft, neutral color scheme of the walls, ceiling, and natural-wood floors is part of their original decor, as are the contemporary white sofa, chrome-and-glass coffee table, and traditional white wing chair. The brown armchair, ladder-back chair, and handsome wood tables represent several refinements in this family's decor. When the warm tones were added to the original white seating group, the look of the whole room became cozier and less formal.

First came the armchair. Several years later, the homeowners supplemented the contemporary coffee table with a century-old drop-leaf table, thus introducing another distinctive element to the decorating scheme. The ladder-back chair and antique writing table in front of the window were part of a third stage.

In short, the room featured here is one that has matured over the past decade or so, without great expense, reorganization, or structural changes. Because the backgrounds and major pieces are easy to live with, thanks to their neutral colors and clean-lined timeless style, they continued to suit the owners, who were able to add just the right touches to provide the new look they wanted.

If you'd like to get a fresh, updated look without making major decorating changes, see Chapter 8—''Fine-Tuning Your Decor''—for more about how seemingly minor redecorating can have major impact. For more about how much background treatments have to do with a room's total impact, see Chapter 4—''Beautiful Backgrounds.''

WHAT STYLE SUITS YOU BEST?

More and more, style is in the mind of the homeowner/decorator as much as it is in the eye of the beholder. One homeowner's casual is another's easygoing contemporary; one's floral upholstered country might be someone else's updated traditional. When you're considering the look you'd like a room to have, what comes to mind first? Is it color, furniture style, texture, pattern, shape? Does your image of an ideal room feature sleek modular seating? Squashy sink-into seating? Natural wood floors? Primitive-patterned area rugs? Do you like wall coverings in rich, deep colors or do you prefer pale tints? If you can find the decorative link that unites your favorite rooms, you'll be well on your way to identifying the decorating style that's right for you.

If you're not 100 percent certain about the look and style you prefer, thumb through decorating publications and visit retail store displays and decorators' showhouses in search of rooms you feel at home in. Once you've found the look you like, studying examples will help you understand a style and guide you in transferring or adapting it to your own home.

Next, consider the all-important contexts of your life-style and budget. If, for instance, you have young children and a fondness for formal traditional furnishings, you may choose to furnish your family room in a modified version of the style, with sturdy reproductions and spill-resistant upholstery. Purchase more costly or fragile items later, or use them for now in a master bedroom or company-only living room.

Keep in mind that seemingly secondary items such as lamps, wall hangings, and window treatments are important when it comes to carrying out a style. The impact and drama of the contemporary living room pictured *at right,* for example, comes as much from bare windows, almost bare walls, and stripped-down lighting as from the tubular chairs and platform seating.

If you've decided that color, fabric, or other aspects are more important to you than a single style, consider an eclectic approach. For more about this, turn the page.

To learn more about deciding on and creating the look you prefer, see Chapter 2— "Expressing Your Own Style." For more about finding items in the styles you've selected, see Chapter 6—"Finding What You Need."

WOULD YOU LIKE TO MIX AND MATCH STYLES?

Most of the time, it's harder *not* to mix styles than it is to settle on just one. What's more, limiting your selections to just one style is usually too narrow an approach. Instead, think in general terms about the mood you'd like a room to convey, then consider elements in terms of their compatibility. The key, of course, is knowing when to mix, when to match, and when to stop.

The mostly contemporary living room pictured *at right* is proof of the power of blending. The rug and sofas are simple, twentieth-century furnishings; an antique cane settee adds an exotic change of pace. Similarly, the blue-gray walls and large-paned French doors are understated and minimally detailed; a carved wooden mantel, painted to look like gray marble, provides an elegant focal point.

Whether mixing comes about because you must build on what you have or you choose to mix because several styles appeal to you, certain guidelines can help make the mix a happy one.

• When you're combining styles, try not to introduce new moods as well. The degree of formality is often the key. A casual old country piece, such as a recycled pine farm table, for example, may go very well with casual contemporary chairs. But neither is likely to be compatible with more formal, highly decorated items, of any style.

• Besides striving to keep the moods of various pieces compatible, try to find other links, too. Color and pattern are great unifiers of furnishings with mixed antecedents. Two or three upolstered chairs of different ages and styles can become a striking and well-matched unit when they're covered in matching or coordinated fabrics.

• Similar or related materials, such as mellow, aged wood or natural woven fabrics, also help bring formerly disparate elements together.

For more about combining the old and the new, see Chapter 5—''Tried-and-True Techniques''—as well as chapters 3 and 7.

DO YOU HAVE THE SPACE TO DO WHAT YOU WANT?

When you think about redecorating, don't let room labels and time-honored uses of space limit your thinking. Although square footage is a constant, carefully chosen and arranged furnishings can do a lot to turn the space you have into the space you want.

Perhaps the most noticeable characteristic of the room pictured *at left* is its multipurpose appeal. It serves as a living room and dining area and also provides a bright setting for several thriving plants.

Despite its versatility, this room isn't large. The way it's put together, however, is a lesson in making the most of what you have. White walls, simply treated windows, and stay-in-the-background carpeting, accented by a pastel rag rug, provide a restful and cohesive setting for the varied furnishings and accessories. Matching tables in the dining area and the conversation corner combine sleek styling with light scale, which helps maintain the airy, spacious look. And there's no room-shrinking clutter.

The seating is comfortable and abundant, yet occupies relatively little visual space. A pair of slender white floor lamps provides ample illumination and blends into the background at the same time, again minimizing the impact of furnishings.

The key to the furnishings' success isn't so much style as scale. The style is an unassuming mix of casual, contemporary, and country. What's important is that no one piece dwarfs its neighbors or its setting. Both the Ludwig Mies van der Rohe-style armchair and the wood-and-rush ottoman/chair combination are see-through pieces rather than solid objects that block the view. The seating area is carefully planned for cozy conversations, with more than adequate traffic space separating it from the dining zone.

For more about tailoring your decor to fit your space, see pages 52-55 and 122-125.

COULD GOOD LIGHTING ADD DRAMA TO YOUR ROOMS?

It's easy to take lighting for granted. Virtually all rooms get some daylight and many boast an overhead fixture that at least keeps you from tripping over the furniture. Add a lamp or two and you can read, sew, and see who you're talking to. But lighting can—and should—be more than strictly utilitarian. With well-planned lighting, you can highlight conversation areas or artworks, bring out the best in a color scheme, feature your home's architectural details, and more.

The two smoothly contemporary rooms pictured here are in the same home. As you can see, the walls, floors, and ceilings are simply treated—almost understated, and with colors that are low-key. In both cases, dramatic overhead lighting, augmented by graceful black metal table lamps, provides much of the visual interest.

The living room pictured *above* is a subtle, neutral-toned setting, offering a variety of textures and materials in place of bright colors. Recessed lighting tucked all around the room's perimeter makes it possible to appreciate all aspects of the room's design and provides an interesting effect of its own as it streaks down the walls.

In the master bedroom, shown *opposite,* a few basic furniture items—the bed, chair, and storage units—take center stage. Track lighting above the bed is general enough to illuminate the entire room; two gooseneck lamps focused on the bed provide excellent reading lights.

Individualized lighting
Track lighting and recessed lighting are both so dramatic in themselves that they're likely to provide considerable interest in your home no matter where you install them. Although we show them here in contemporary settings, that doesn't

mean that updated overhead lighting won't work in more traditional surroundings, too. Consider, for example, using brass-finished or softly colored canisters to bring this contemporary lighting style closer to your home's decorative character.

Keep in mind, too, that many other types of lighting also can add a special touch to your room. Wall sconces and chandeliers, available in a wide range of styles and materials, can do wonders for a country or colonial setting; unusual table or floor lamps can serve as style statements as well as lighting.

For more about the decorative aspects of lighting, see pages 56-57 and 134-137.

WHAT CAN ACCESSORIES DO FOR A ROOM?

Accessories are among the things that give a room its essential character. The accent items you choose should reflect your personality, and give pleasure for years to come. The point is not to fill up empty wall and table spaces, but to provide charm and give the whole space a well-put-together air. More than almost any other features, accessories reflect the individual tastes of whoever put them on display. They're communicators, mood-setters, and generally indispensable parts of any decorating scheme.

The window-walled dining room pictured *at right* is all of a piece, with mellow wood furnishings, Mexican adobe tile flooring, and vertical board walls each contributing their own relaxed, Old World charm. Without the wall-hung woven baskets and the intricately patterned antique blue-and-white ware on the hutch, however, much of the room's distinctive look would be gone.

What you consider an appropriate accessory for any room in your home is up to you. A child's first kindergarten painting, mounted in a simple metal frame, can add as much to a living room as an expensive lithograph. The important thing is that whatever you hang on your walls, display on your shelves, and arrange on your coffee table should reflect your tastes and interests.

Because accessories are often less costly than other decorative components, you can use them to emphasize or even modify a style. Adding contemporary wall hangings or artwork, for example, to a room furnished mainly with traditional pieces can provide a refreshing update. And the cost is likely to be much less than for purchasing a new sofa or chair in a more contemporary style.

Because accessories are so varied, there are no hard-and-fast rules that apply to their purchase, arrangement, or use. For some starting-out ideas, however, see Chapter 8. For more about accessorizing enough but not too much, see Chapter 10—"When To Stop." And for accessories you can make yourself, turn to Chapter 9—"Sewing for Your Home."

DO YOU NEED THE HELP OF A DESIGN PROFESSIONAL?

Decorating your home is a highly personal activity. It's also one that calls for considerable self-confidence, creativity, imagination, resourcefulness—and sometimes more time than you can give it. If you're faced with a decorating project that you can't quite pull together on your own, think about consulting a design professional. The extent and expense of design services vary tremendously, so no matter what your budget and circumstances, you should be able to find the advice and adviser to meet your needs.

When you look around the room or rooms you'd like to "do something with," you may have an image in your mind of the look you'd like to create, but no firm idea about how to achieve that look. Or you may not be quite sure what styles and types of furnishings would make the most of the setting. Perhaps you need someone to give you an overall picture of what *could* be done to make your home look its best, so that you can adapt some of the ideas as your budget allows. One of the biggest assets of a designer is that he or she can help eliminate costly mistakes. Also, the designer can often show you (or tell you where to find) fabrics or furniture that you might not have access to on your own.

For help with these and other decorating quandaries, books, magazines, and other sources can go only so far. Sometimes, you need in-person advice.

The sophisticated efficiency apartment shown on these two pages illustrates how a designer and homeowner can work together not only to make the space comfortable and functional, but also to give it individual style. The owner wanted a quiet oasis away from a busy professional life—a place

with serene colors, flexible furniture, and sophisticated flair. Working jointly, they chose neutral, but high-fashion gray for the background. To make the best use of the space, the designer suggested such things as the L-shape seating group tucked into the corner and the two small, easily movable coffee tables. The marble-topped dining table they selected also doubles for games or office work, and the chairs can pull over to the conversation area when needed. Track lighting provides soft general illumination, and highlights special features like the Chinese screen hung over the sofa. Through their combined efforts, they were able to achieve exactly the effect the owner wanted.

You may think of professional design advice as something that only people with ambitious decorating projects and ample budgets can afford. It's true that full-scale design services—planning an entire home and supervising purchases of items ranging from sofas to candlesticks—are costly. It's important to realize, however, that there are ways to utilize a designer's services on a smaller scale. For more about the range of services provided by professionals, see pages 104-105.

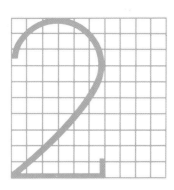

2

EXPRESSING YOUR OWN STYLE

Country, traditional, contemporary—we're all used to labels for the rooms we see in furniture stores or other people's homes. Like many labels, style categories are helpful in identifying different approaches to decorating, but these labels are only one way to define style. Equally important is the way a room feels to you and others. A contemporary setting, for example, might seem casual, elegant, dramatic—or a combination of all three. This chapter can help you shape the established decorating categories into expressions of your own special style.

WELCOME-HOME ROOMS

Home is—or should be—a welcoming place you look forward to returning to. What's more, a room that welcomes you will, in all probability, do the same for your guests.

Walk into the room pictured here and you're likely to feel at home right away. Homey elements include the familiar styling of rolled-arm and wing-back seating, and soft blue upholstery prints that create serenity without being bland or boring.

Reassuringly familiar as the upholstered furniture is in its country-traditional dress, it could have much the same effect using very different fabrics. For example, contemporary patterns, earth-tone natural fabrics, even bright solids, all have places in a room that blends the past and the present into a seamless whole.

There's more than one unifying theme in this room, however. The blue used on the major seating pieces is a key, but the warm glow of the wood floor, tables, and armoire plays an equally important part. In virtually any home, the mellow glow of golden oak and the honey-hued patina of pine add their own welcoming warmth.

Textures, too, have a lot to do with the appeal of this sunlit space. The nubby rag rug, woven baskets, casually arranged pillows, and well-chosen extras provide pleasing counterpoints.

Accents also play a vital role. Items that reflect your taste and life-style may be more contemporary, larger, brighter, or different in other ways from the calico rabbit, elegant tea set, and ceramic lamps used here. The important thing is that the accents you choose have meaning for you. After all, that's what home is all about. *(continued)*

WELCOME-HOME ROOMS
(continued)

As the picture on the preceding page shows, the old and familiar have their own strong and special appeal. Inviting spaces, however, can result from the blending of any number of diverse elements. Generally speaking, if you like the pieces individually, you can find a way to make them work together.

Start by looking for common denominators among seemingly unrelated pieces. Color, texture, and scale can provide subtle yet effective links between pieces that at first glance don't match.

For example, woods that are in the same color range are also often compatible, regardless of the style of the pieces themselves. That's part of what makes the eclectic dining room pictured *at right* work so well. The bentwood chairs are well suited to the maple parsons table, not only because both are simply, though differently, styled, but also because the woods are compatible. Similarly, an old claw-foot dining table of oak can happily share space with younger-generation chairs made of pine or beech.

The clean-lined, wood-warmed dining room pictured *above* also combines a variety of elements into a delightfully cohesive whole. Here, the pieces reflect a certain unity of age and style—in this case, country colonial. Their simple shapes go well with each other, although they were collected over a period of years.

The same rules of relationships that apply to large pieces of furniture work for accessories, too. In the photo *above,* such accessories as the wooden hen on the blanket chest against the wall and the colorful hooked rug in the center of the room provide variety and at the same time augment the mood set by the furniture. Look for items that have something in common, whether that something is the material, the color, the shape, or the function. An ornate brass chandelier, for example, can shine equally well in the company of colonial-style brass candlesticks or angular brass frames around contemporary posters.

This combine-and-conquer approach has more than creative and aesthetic advantages: It's economical as well. You can use what you have, buy a few new pieces, and create a harmonious room that owes its unity and appeal to your own design sense.

PURE
AND
SIMPLE

Simplicity comes in many ages, sizes, and styles. Contemporary furnishings have no monopoly on straightforward lines and clean detailing. In fact, an unadorned nineteenth-century Shaker table and its simple-verging-on-stark twentieth-century equivalent have a lot in common. Whenever and wherever the origins of such furnishings, a simply furnished room can be soothing, serene, self-sufficient, and functional. It may look like a carefully composed still life, but chances are it's also eminently livable.

One of the advantages of a keep-it-simple philosophy is that you need fewer elements than you might think to make it work. In rooms where you can't see the forest for the trees, valued possessions get lost in the crowd. But in a well-edited room, everything works, and everything is noticed. Just as a single rose in a bud vase can be as decorative as an elaborate floral arrangement, a room furnished with only a few simple, carefully chosen pieces can be a perfect example of grace and elegance.

The colonial-flavored room pictured *at left* is a good example of how this minimalist approach can be applied to any decorative style. The richly colored Oriental rug accents the polished wood-strip floor; an ancestral portrait highlights one white-painted wall; and a cohesive collection of pewter tableware brightens the classic corner cupboard. The dining table and chairs serve as the centerpiece, which is topped by a daisy-filled basket as down-to-earth and basic as the room itself.

The principles illustrated by the colonial furnishings and accessories in this room span the centuries and styles. To sum them up briefly:
• Condense accessories into a prominently displayed single collection. Or choose one or two major accessories in place of many small ones.
• Avoid sharp contrasts in materials, textures, and colors. Subdued colors on walls and woodwork automatically focus attention on furniture and accessories.
• Furniture with graceful lines, simple shapes, and surfaces free of elaborate carvings and sharp edges is the key to successful simplicity.

(continued)

PURE
AND
SIMPLE
(continued)

Back to basics doesn't mean down with details. As the wood-and-white living room shown on these two pages proves, the simpler the setting, the more important the details.

Here, puffy white pillows and well-padded upholstery contrast dramatically with unadorned wood floors. The virtually monochromatic color schemes and the interesting combination of textured fabrics and smooth wood take precedence over color and pattern. Using the same fabric over and over again creates instant continuity; painting the walls, ceiling, and woodwork to match simplifies the approach further. Accessories and details add a special quality to this simply furnished space, inviting the eye to linger on artifacts, antiques, and art.

The Scandinavian wedding chairs (traditionally, carved by a father for his daughter before her marriage), carefully lined up along a wall in the adjoining sun-room, have a visual distinction all their own.

They're dark in a light setting, old in a contemporary one. They're compatible with the other wood pieces, but just different enough to add drama to the whole assemblage.

Strategic planning
With a neutral background such as the one illustrated here, it's easy to change the focus of the room. Add a brightly colored rug and you get one effect; add a wall hanging or a simple yet striking window treatment and you get another. Rearrange two pieces of furniture and the room's apparent shape may change. You can replace pieces as their appeal begins to pall and reinstate them when they're welcome again.

As the photographs here and on the preceding two pages show, simplicity isn't the hallmark of any one period or style. Nor does it have only one price tag. Simplicity can be luxurious or economical, old or new, a combination of many price ranges, ages, and styles, or representative of just one.

EXPRESSING YOUR OWN STYLE

TIMELESS HERITAGE

A style that's classic, whether it has its roots in past centuries or our own, is timeless. Just as many styles from the distant past have survived in easily recognizable form in contemporary homes, so have more recent styles. As you'll see on the following pages, so-called "modern" furnishings also can convey a sense of permanence and connection between the past, present, and future.

The gracious master bedroom pictured *at right* clearly contains much of the past, but it's by no means a museum setting. The pencil-post bed, birchwood chest, Windsor chair, and barrel-back cupboard are all time-honored and familiar pieces, as at home in this twentieth-century setting as they were generations ago.

The cupboard wasn't originally a bedroom piece, of course, and its use here illustrates a key technique in bringing the past into the present—adaptation. You can adapt an old piece in its original form for use in a way not originally intended—or even thought of—in its early days. Or you, or a manufacturer, can modify a style for present-day use. The main thing is to disregard the rigid limitations of use and style that might keep you from getting the most possible enjoyment and benefit from a given item. An old oak icebox, for example, can house your stereo system, or a daybed could become a living room sofa.

Remember, too, that not only can you mix "old" furniture of various ages and styles, but you also can use newer pieces with older ones. An accessory of any period can look fine in a past-dominated room, if the mood and general style are right. For example, the mini-slat blinds used in the bedroom pictured here are centuries removed from most of the other items in the room. Yet the simplicity of this understated and very practical window treatment is perfectly in keeping with the restrained elegance that characterizes the decor.

(continued)

EXPRESSING
YOUR OWN
STYLE

**TIMELESS
HERITAGE**
(continued)

All classics were "modern" once. Just because the room pictured *at left* is furnished in a way never dreamed of a hundred years ago doesn't make it any less timeless. The shapes are simple, the lines clean, the colors welcoming. Its place in history is as secure as that of the burnished-wood dining room shown *above,* though 150 years separate the basic designs.

The "new classic" living room dates back to the late 1920s, when architect Ludwig Mies van der Rohe introduced a line of furniture that relied on leather, glass, and chrome-plated steel. His Barcelona chair and table (named after the city in which they were first exhibited) have survived in unmodified form to this day, and have served as inspiration for a new generation of frankly functional furniture.

Other elements in this room were carefully selected to carry forward the furniture's spare, geometric lines. A quartet of bright blue prints were hung to be viewed from a seated position. Clear glass accessories augment the table's transparency. Track-mounted canister lights illuminate the art and a single, tree-size ficus.

The dining room harks back to pre-Revolutionary times. Here, pine and poplar vintage furnishings are accented by a collection of yellowware pottery and stoneware jugs. Candles provide mood lighting.

You needn't have an attic full of family heirlooms or invest in costly designer originals to create your own classic and distinctive decor. Concentrate on buying well-designed furniture that you like and can afford. Just a few well-loved pieces can set the stage for a whole room's worth of personal history.

HANDCRAFTED
APPEAL

Things made by hand seem friendlier than the same objects made by machine. No matter who created an item— or when it was crafted —handmade furnishings and accessories bring personalized warmth to a home. You probably already have a few favorite handcrafts that serve as accents— but if you're especially interested in old artifacts, or fascinated by contemporary crafts, why not build an entire decorating scheme around them?

One of the great delights of handcrafts lies with their acquisition. Whether it's a flea-market treasure you came upon during a vacation, a basket you purchased from an artisan at a regional crafts fair, or ceramics sought out in a potter's studio, the memories that a handmade object evokes are almost as important as the object itself.

The country kitchen pictured *above* reflects years of collecting handcrafted treasures. Antique pewter and crockery brighten an eighteenth-century pine cupboard along one wall. The dining table and chairs, as well as the tilt-top hutch table in the background, are also handmade. The kinds of items

we more often think of as handcrafts are well represented here, too, by the braided rug, hand-woven cloth and napkins, and rush seats on the chairs.

The dining room featured *opposite* is also rich in handcrafted items that trace their ancestry back to an earlier period of America's history. Here, a pine corner cupboard, homespun blankets, a Shaker basket, a rustic woven wreath, and hand-carved decoys

combine their textures and individual charms into a cohesive setting that proudly announces its origins.

Keep in mind, too, that you yourself can make a variety of items that may be a great source of pride for years to come. Skills such as stenciling, drying flowers, braiding rugs, weaving baskets and building furniture are as appealing as ever—and so are their end results. Many crafts projects are available in kit form for those who'd like to try to create their own handcrafts but aren't yet quite sure of their abilities.   *(continued)*

HANDCRAFTED APPEAL

(continued)

Almost by definition, most antiques, whatever their style, period, or place of origin, are handcrafted. You might not think, for example, of the formal, highly polished furniture made for wealthy city dwellers centuries ago as handcrafts, but they were certainly made by hand.

More in tune with the handmade look as we think of it today are country-style antiques, made of locally available materials and usually for people of more modest means. Solid, unpretentious, and durable, their aura of informality makes them compatible with most other styles of furniture and virtually all architectural moods. Like folk art, folk furniture can set the decorating tone for a room or even an entire house, as the two restful rooms pictured here illustrate.

The living room shown *at right* combines a variety of handmade Spanish and Mexican pieces with casual, contemporary seating for an effect that is harmonious—and eminently livable. Wood-plank floors and a ceiling beamed with pine poles called *vigas* provide clear indication of the room's country spirit. Woven-seat chairs, an antique painted table, an elaborately ornamented trunk, and a boldly displayed assemblage of antlers contribute to the room's special, one-of-a-kind charm.

In the same home, the simple yet sophisticated bedroom pictured *above* also boasts an appealing collection of handcrafted furniture—some old, some new. The four-poster, for example, is a brand-new custom-made version of an antique bed. However, the paired bedside tables, rubbed with sagebrush-green paint to emphasize their Southwestern origins, are as old as they look.

EXPRESSING YOUR OWN STYLE

MIXING AND MATCHING

Just as there's no one "correct" skirt length anymore, there's no "only" way to choose, use, or combine furnishings. That's not to say you shouldn't decide on a unifying theme—color, pattern, or fabric, perhaps. It's just that variety and imagination are as important as anything else. The key to good decorating is to choose what you like, in whatever range of styles you like, and use it in the way that looks best to you.

An eclectic room that works is one in which each piece has been chosen on its own merits. Items may come from many places and be either old or new, but if they work well together, they probably have something in common—such as country origins, natural materials, or one or two striking colors used as accents on one piece and key mood-setters on another.

The well-assorted living room shown *at right* is an example of bold selection that brings out the best in its setting. Architectural details in this room date back to the early part of the century and set an opulent mood. The fireplace, complete with its original mantel, provides an ideal focal point for the room; the rich finish of the woodwork calls out for equally rich tones in the furnishings.

To take advantage of these built-in assets, the owners created a conversation area around the fireplace. Depending on where guests sit, they have a view of the fireplace, the bay windows, or the intriguing detailing on other woodwork in the room.

The furnishings themselves reflect the same careful selection as their arrangement does. The sofa, upholstered in brown velvet, and the dramatic nail-studded armchair, covered in black leather, are both about the same age as the house itself. A pair of tan leather Barcelona chairs—the same contemporary classic design shown on pages 32 and 33— face the sofa. Simple lines, subdued colors, and classic origins unify the three types of seating. An Oriental rug adds bright color to the neutral-dominated setting.

(continued)

MIXING AND MATCHING

(continued)

A first glance, it may seem that the elegant living room pictured *at right* is a classic example of formal antique decorating. An elegant fireplace flanked by floor-to-ceiling columns, a jewel-toned Oriental rug, and gilt-framed pictures carefully arranged in formal rows all contribute to that first impression.

But look again, and the room takes on a much more individual air. The paintings are watercolors, found in an antique shop in southern France. The rush-seated ladder-back chairs, country-style rather than formal city-built antiques, are also secondhand finds. White sofas, although carefully aligned beside the fireplace, are designed for everyday living—they're covered in a durable, stain-resistant fabric. Bright yellow walls enliven the tranquil atmosphere, as do the cheerfully informal toss pillows. Thanks to these combinations and counterbalancings, the room offers the best of old and new, formal and informal.

Finding your own best way

Eclectic decorating gives you more options and fewer limitations than most other approaches do. It lets you live with the furnishings you like best. The other side of the coin, of course, is that you do have to decide what each piece is worth to you as an element in your own highly personalized setting.

If you're starting from the beginning, your main task is to decide what kinds of pieces you need—seating, storage, and so forth. Then establish financial priorities, and buy what you need as you can afford it, keeping both spontaneity and the importance of some cohesive quality in mind.

If you're working with what you have and would like to create a more personalized look, the first thing to do is take stock of all your furnishings. If there are items you've never quite liked, perhaps now's the time to store them, donate them to charity, or have a garage sale. This may leave gaps in your room, so you may well find yourself shopping for a few key pieces. Again, keep some overall theme in mind as you shop. Consider what you like about the furnishings you've kept—bright colors, perhaps, or natural materials. Look for new pieces that will fit in or will provide the one striking accent that could make the whole room special.

SOFT AND ROMANTIC

You may not consider yourself a romantic, but there's room in everyone's life—and home— for a little romance. No matter how tailored your den or how twenty-first-century your kitchen, it's nice to have at least one room where the hard edges are softened, the bright colors muted, and the mood mellowed. You can't always flee to a windswept beach at sunset or curl up in a firelit living room on a snowy afternoon, but as you'll see on these pages and the two that follow, you *can* turn a corner or room of your home into a romantic refuge.

Ruffles and flourishes are all very well, but not everyone feels comfortable with them, or looks right surrounded by them. That doesn't rule out romantic decorating, however.

In the subtly romantic bedroom pictured *at right,* for example, soft colors, appealing textures, and simple lines combine to create an undeniably romantic but never fussy retreat. The white laminate platform bed is thoroughly contemporary; the bedclothes, more subtle. The geometric pattern of the linens, up-to-date though it is, becomes charmingly ageless thanks to an unexpected use of pastels rather than earth tones or brilliant primary colors for the concentric squares.

The room's pale yellow walls and sunshiny interior shutters add a touch of country-inn charm, accented by a basket of brightly colored flowers and a willow wreath. Other accessories, notably the old apothecary chest, duck decoys, and family photograph, add a touch of gentle nostalgia to the setting.

If this room has the kind of subtly romantic look that appeals to you, there are several lessons to be applied. Start with the colors. Pastels and other muted hues are easy on the eye and naturally soothing, as this multi-pastel room illustrates.

Texture and shape are important, too. Round off angular corners if you can; use satin-finish paints and well-padded furniture, rather than high-gloss enamels and tightly tailored pieces. Abundant pillows and loosely woven or quilted fabrics are also key contributors to an understated romantic look. *(continued)*

SOFT AND ROMANTIC

(continued)

The room pictured *at right* and the detail shown *above* present classic romantic images, starting with the floral fabric and continuing with the candles, carved mantel, and gracefully draped French doors. But the romance of the past is as much a part of this room's mood as is the more conventional romantic image of ruffles and flowers and lots of pink paint. Tall French doors, embellished by draperies in a fabric that matches the upholstery and tablecloth, add to the mood. Even such seemingly minor details as the graceful brass handles are integral parts of the setting.

In the sitting room shown here, the nineteenth-century pine chest, dainty end table, and well-dressed coffee table are all relics of an English-country-house past that we know from books, movies, and television. Adding color and still more charm to this setting are the heavy linen canvas floorcloth painted to look like

an Aubusson carpet, silhouettes atop the elegant mantel, and graceful candlesticks placed at strategic intervals around the room.

Bread and roses

Dreams of historic houses and mythical heroes aside, there's a lot of present-day practicality here, too. The rose-spattered fabric covering the love seat and table and framing the doorway is a bold, bright pattern; it's far removed from the small-scale pastels traditionally associated with country-house romantic decorating. The walls are plain, though pink—and they're sensibly coated with practical, easy-to-apply latex. The white bowl, pitcher, and accessories in the small photograph and on the table featured *at right* are certainly in keeping with the romantic mood, but they're sturdy, new, and intended to be used as well as admired.

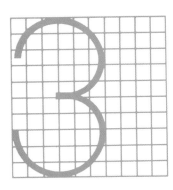

PLANNING DECORATING CHANGES

Sooner or later, any room begins to look the worse for wear—or begins to wear on you. Maybe some furnishings are fraying around the edges, or perhaps the overall effect simply doesn't suit your taste or life-style any longer. Whatever your reasons for redecorating, this chapter will lead you step by step through the process of giving a room an entirely new look without replacing all of its contents.

ANALYZING WHAT YOU HAVE

Take a look at the living room pictured *at right.* Pretty—and far from threadbare—its soft, traditional look and monochromatic color scheme had become a bit too sedate for its owners, whose tastes had changed over the years. On the next few pages, we'll show you how fresh paint, fabric, lighting, accessories, and window treatments transformed the room, making it an attractive reflection of one couple's aesthetic evolution. More important, we'll translate this successful redecorating into adaptable, step-by-step tactics that you can call upon for help in carrying out your own room-renewal project.

Why do you want to redecorate?
Before you begin making nitty-gritty decisions, sit back, put your feet up, and relax in the room you plan to change. Take time to assess its pluses and minuses so that you clearly understand *why* you want to redecorate in the first place.

Are some furniture pieces in need of repair or replacement? Or do you simply dislike them? Are the furnishings out of touch with your day-to-day living needs? Do the colors of paints and fabrics still please you? Is the specific decorating style in tune with your desires, or has your taste changed over the years? Also consider the room's general mood. Is it too formal or too casual? Are you longing for a change to airy brightness—or cozy intimacy?

Once you've listed the room's decorative pros and cons and made notes describing the style and mood you hope to create, you're well on your way to a successful new decorating scheme.

PLANNING DECORATING CHANGES

GETTING STARTED

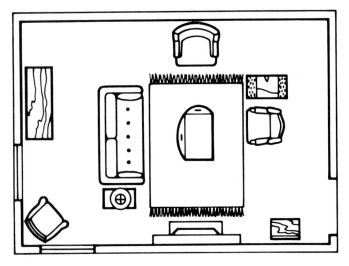

Planning and carrying out a successful decorating project isn't a simple matter of running out and buying a roomful of new furnishings. In fact, such a "quick fix" approach, temporarily satisfying as it may be, often leaves you dissatisfied and disappointed in the long run.

To be sure you're on the right track in planning changes, start by understanding how you want to use the rooms in question. Do you want a quiet sitting room or a lively family gathering spot? What activities must be accommodated here? Do reading, bill paying, homework, TV watching, dining, and hobbies all need niches? Do your present furnishings answer those needs or are there some furniture gaps to fill?

What's your style?
Now try to pin down the "look" you want. Start with a stack of decorating magazines and clip out photographs of rooms that appeal to you. After you've assembled several clippings, spread them out on the floor and analyze what they have in common. It may be as obvious as a specific decorat-

ing or furniture style (country, contemporary, or traditional), or a certain color scheme.

The common thread linking most of your clippings may be less tangible—a special mood that transcends narrow style categories. Are you lured by intimate rooms or wide-open ones? Do you prefer spaces that are filled with eye-catching mementos, or would you be more comfortable in a sophisticated room with a minimum of clutter? Have you clipped rooms that are basically formal or informal?

Also visit furniture stores and decorator showcase houses and take note of room settings that you particularly like. Also, think about the homes of friends and neighbors. What do you like and dislike about their decorating schemes? In whose home do you feel most comfortable—and *why*?

Be true to yourself
A final note: Once you've settled on a look, stick to it. Don't be swayed by here-today-gone-tomorrow furnishings fads. After all, this is *your* home. Let it become a one-of-a-kind expression of *your* taste, interests, and creativity.

48

DECIDING WHAT TO KEEP AND WHAT TO CHANGE

Once you've charted your general decorating course, you're ready to get down to specifics. This is the time to decide which furnishings to keep, which to discard, and what items can be face-lifted to enhance your new decorating scheme.

The goal of the redecorating project featured in this chapter was to move from a formal, traditional look to a casual, country air. Most of the original major furnishings—the upholstered seating pieces, armoire, brass lamp, decoys, primitive wooden box, and ladder-back chair—can stay; they'll work either as is or adapt to suit the new look. A few items—the colonial pewterware, ancestral portrait, lamp table, and butler's tray table (shown in front of the sofa that's pictured on pages 46 and 47)—will have to go.

To help effect a major change of scene, the color scheme was updated, too. The goal: an airy yet down-to-earth mood with an emphasis on neutrals and natural woods.

When you're undertaking a redecorating project of this magnitude—or even a smaller one—a little instant gratification will keep you motivated. Here, some easy and dramatic changes got the project off the ground quickly. Simply repainting the green walls crisp white worked wonders, inexpensively opening up a once-dark room. New track lighting also helped to expand space by bouncing welcome light off the walls.

To foster a natural, warm look, the room's painted woodwork was stripped, chairs were reupholstered in soft sherbet shades, and one wall was accented with a subtle, pinstripe wall covering.

As we noted on the preceding page, a seemingly simple change of background can yield big visual results. Here, you see those dramatic changes in process. Beautiful oak ceiling moldings, window trim, and the fireplace—long hidden under coats of paint—are now stripped to their natural, wood-grained beauty. The once-green walls, which enclosed the room a little too snugly, seem to recede when freshened with white paint.

Backgrounds in brief

A change of background will give even the same old furnishings a surprisingly different look. The important thing to remember is: Light colors recede and dark ones advance. To put that to use in your home, opt for strong or dark colors on the walls, floor, and ceiling when you want to cozy up a room. Conversely, choose white or light colors when you want a room to seem larger.

Background treatments also can alter the apparent proportions of a room. For instance, you can lower a too-high ceiling with a dark or bright color, or "raise the roof" with white paint. If a long, narrow room is your problem, minimize its tunneled look by painting one or both end walls a strong color.

Let your background color play up architectural assets or minimize flaws. Highlight an ornate fireplace or special woodwork by painting it to contrast with the walls. Or, make awkwardly placed doors disappear by painting or papering them to match the walls.

For more about choosing just the right background treatments for your rooms, see Chapter 4—"Beautiful Backgrounds."

INTRODUCING
KEY ELEMENTS

Once the backgrounds are completed, it's time to replace or refurbish some old furnishings. That's what the partially furnished room shown *opposite* illustrates. The photograph *at left* focuses on some of the new key materials and colors.

Because the original sofa was in good condition and had simple, pleasing lines, it was saved and reupholstered in a white-on-white patterned fabric. A pastel mini-print fabric, echoing the raspberry stripe in the wallpaper, renews the old wing chair and adds an appealing touch of color.

Color considerations

If you're trying to decide what colors and patterns to introduce into your redecorating project, a few guidelines apply.
• Use warm colors when you want an exciting, stimulating environment, cool ones when serenity is your goal.
• Let warm hues "heat up" a cool, north-facing room or one that receives little natural light. Conversely, refresh rooms that receive an abundance of sunlight with cool blues, greens, or purples.
• Turn to patterns when you want coziness; minimize them and depend more on solids when you're working toward an open, airy mood.

When it comes to picking a specific color scheme, one of the surest routes to success is to let a favorite piece of artwork or fabric inspire you, then let the proportions as well as the color of whatever object you're using as inspiration be

your guide. For instance, if a particular fabric is your inspiration, choose one of the paler, quieter hues from the design for the largest areas of your room—the walls and ceiling, and perhaps the floor. Choose one of the pattern's bolder colors for large upholstered pieces. Finally use the sharpest color sparingly in artwork and accessories.

Fail-safe schemes

If you lack confidence in your ability to work with color, try one of these three reliable types of combinations.
• *Related,* or *analogous,* schemes consist of colors that are close to each other on the color wheel. Start with your favorite color. If that color is blue, for example, you'd build on it with related blue-green and green accents. If you start with orange, you'd be safe to add yellow-orange and yellow accents.
• *Neutral* schemes, which include large proportions of whites, beiges, browns, grays, and taupes, are naturally harmonious. Textures, such as knotty woods, smooth glass and metal, nubby fabrics, and woven wicker, keep neutral rooms from becoming bland.
• *One-color-plus-white* is a guaranteed success. Such high-contrast schemes often use white as the major element, with a bright color used as the accent; bolder versions might have a bright color dominating the scene, relieved by white accents.

PLANNING DECORATING CHANGES

BRINGING IN LIGHT

As you can see, this updated decorating scheme relies on a crisp, one-shade-plus-white color scheme. Without good lighting, however, this light-hearted color scheme would never be seen to its best advantage.

Illuminating ideas

When you choose lighting, don't limit yourself to the same old lamps. Instead, experiment with some different ideas. Start with lamps for reading and other tasks, then supplement that light with specialty fixtures. A strip or two of track lighting, for example, could wash walls with light or spotlight artwork or other prized possessions.

Consider tucking uplights or torchères into one or two corners; their dramatic beams will open up formerly dark areas and also "push up" the ceiling by bouncing light off it.

Small, clamp-on spotlights are affordable and fun, too. Clamp them to shelves, pots of indoor trees, artwork frames, or the top of a tall armoire or secretary.

Maximizing daylight

If reinforcing a light and natural mood is your goal, be sure to use light-admitting window treatments. A trim mini-blind, pleated shade, or lattice panels like those shown here also will enhance spaciousness since they take up no floor space.

The lattice panels in this room provide partial daytime privacy yet still admit ample light. At night, ordinary roller shades mounted inside the window casings pull down for greater privacy. Most important, the homemade panels play up the country mood, adding old-fashioned, porch-like nostalgia to the setting.

ARRANGING THE PIECES

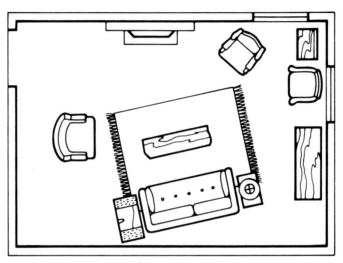

Building your background, refurbishing furnishings, and working with color are not the complete redecorating story. Making your redecorated room work depends as much on room arrangement as on the elements we've already discussed.

Although the arrangement pictured *at far right* is not yet accessorized, the major pieces have been placed to make the room comfortable for daily living. The green armoire that appears earlier in the chapter has been stripped and refinished; an old wooden bench has joined the scene to serve as a bucolic coffee table.

In the final room plan shown *at top right,* the sofa is angled slightly to give the rectangular room a more interesting perspective. The upholstered armchair nestled nearby creates a pleasant conversation grouping. Placed in cozy proximity to the fireplace, the wing chair makes an inviting place to read or just relax.

With flexible furnishings like these, a number of different room plans are possible. The variation shown *at center right,* for example, allows the sofa and two upholstered chairs to gather before the focal-point fireplace. In this plan, the armoire creates symmetry and balance when positioned directly opposite the fireplace. A second alternative, shown *at bottom right,* positions the sofa and two upholstered chairs on a strong diagonal that visually widens the room. Here, the armoire moves to the lefthand wall.

In each plan, furnishings are grouped to form logical traffic paths into and out of the doorway at left. As the furnishings are repositioned, track canisters can be redirected to provide light wherever it's needed.

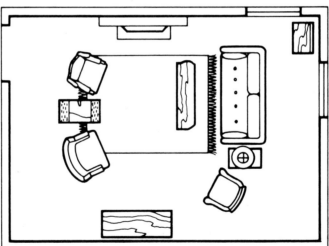

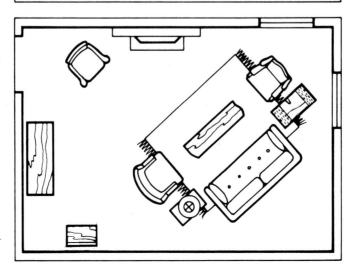

PLANNING DECORATING CHANGES

COMPLETING THE LOOK

Here's our featured room, complete with accessories chosen to augment the natural, down-home mood. The setting illustrates how personal accents can add the finishing touches to any scheme.

The original pair of decoys became a flock, with new wooden shorebirds displayed on the bench-turned-coffee-table. Next to the wing chair, a weather vane adds whimsical charm. Organic baskets, plants, and dried weeds reinforce the back-to-nature theme. Finally, a miniature Oriental screen above the mantel plays up the new color scheme.

Tying accessories together

As you'd imagine from the intriguing display pictured *at right,* fine-tuning your room may be the most enjoyable part of your redecorating project. Let your accessories be a true reflection of who you really are. If that means filling a wall with a display of kids' watercolors, so be it; if it necessitates lining every wall in a room with book-laden shelves, that's fine, too.

One of the best ways to give your accessories impact is to display them in cohesive groupings. A collection of figurines, for example, can easily fade into the background if each piece is displayed separately. Group such items together on one table or shelf, however, and they'll make an instant impression.

You also can pick a fairly general theme—say, Oriental accents—and display items together, or assemble pieces made of the same material, whether porcelain, wood, or glass. If your treasures are unrelated, consider grouping them by color. For more about accessorizing, see Chapter 8.

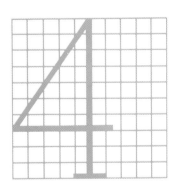

4

BEAUTIFUL BACKGROUNDS

Whether you choose richly colored or patterned walls, mood-setting floors or ceilings, or handsome focal-point window coverings, make the most of your backgrounds. Although a neutral backdrop can be wonderfully serene, there are times when you want more punch and excitement. This chapter—plus your own imagination and courage—can help you turn ho-hum walls, ceilings, floors, and windows into bold, eye-catching accents.

Many people shy away from boldly colored walls for fear that they'll upstage a room's furniture and accessories. Used correctly, however, strong wall colors can serve deftly as supporting players that enhance the items they surround.

Nearly any wall color will work in the right setting. Just be sure that the color is compatible with the feeling you expect the room to convey. Do you want low-key restfulness? Crisp, high-contrast punch? A bright, sunny look, or a cool, refreshing feeling? If you're unsure, take a tip from the previous chapter and go through lots of decorating magazines, clipping photos of rooms that "feel" right to you. You'll probably discover threads of colorful similarities tying them all together—fresh, warm colors that remind you of a favorite flower garden; sunny yellows that give you a special lift; cool, shady greens and blues; or mellow earth tones that are easy to live with.

In the handsome living room pictured *at right,* jade-green walls infuse the room with a freshness that's both exciting and restful. The wall color not only establishes the Oriental-style serenity that this homeowner wanted, but it also echoes the greens found in the room's striking Far Eastern accessories.

Ample doses of white or light tones will help keep a strong wall color like this from darkening your rooms or overpowering your furnishings. Here, plain off-white sofas, crisp, white-painted woodwork and ceilings, and a creamy area rug provide the needed relief. To pull the green-and-white scheme together, the rug sports a simple border of deep green.

(continued)

Patterned walls are especially effective mood-setters, and one of the easiest ways to add pattern is with wall coverings, which also can disguise damaged wall surfaces and blend awkward architectural features into the background. In addition, many coverings offer matching and coordinating fabrics that make it easy for amateurs to create a unified decorating scheme. Best of all, there's a wide range of well-designed wall coverings available today.

Use an appealing wall covering as the starting point of a decorating scheme. Or install a wall covering to strengthen a mood that's already established. The cottagelike floral print in the girl's bedroom pictured *opposite* reinforces the country-style ambience of the room and also echoes its red accents. In a small space like this one, it's usually best to stick to small-scale prints on a white or light-color ground.

Try your hand at stenciling

Stenciling, an art that flourished during colonial times when wallpapers were scarce and costly, is back in fashion. Using precut stencil kits, or your own one-of-a-kind designs, you can create charming borders for doors and windows, friezes, or allover patterns to suit any mood or color scheme. With a little practice, any novice can stencil a wall. To create your own stencil, make a pattern, then cut it out of commercial stencil

paper. Secure the stencil to the wall with masking tape, then carefully dab paint through the stencil, using a nearly dry paint brush. (Too much paint on your brush may result in runny, uneven results.)

The owners of the bedroom shown *above* designed their own rolling leaf-and-flower frieze. A related design—a geometric bar-and-flower motif—creates vertical bands that emphasize architectural assets, such as the circa-1860 window treatments.

CEILINGS

Look up! You'll probably find a ceiling that's begging for a touch of your decorative creativity. White or off-white is always a good, safe choice, especially for rooms with low ceilings. But why limit yourself? Let a dramatic treatment of strong, solid colors, painted or papered designs, patterned tiles, or warm wood crown your rooms. Before choosing a ceiling design, understand your goals. Do you want to create coziness or airiness? Do you want to play up or deemphasize an unusual ceiling angle? With a little imagination, you can create any effect you like.

A fanciful, trellised ceiling lends romantic, gazebo-style fun to the inviting bedroom pictured *above*. Although the lighthearted ceiling and matching columns look hand-painted, they really consist of wallpaper panels. This *trompe l'oeil* ("fool-the-eye") effect not only imbues the room with gardenlike style, it also helps play up a coved ceiling.

When you opt for a patterned ceiling such as this one, it's usually best to keep your walls and floors simple by using solid colors. Here, creamy-white walls and natural sisal carpet slip discreetly into the background.

You can create your own trompe l'oeil ceilings by using wall coverings with realistic, three-dimensional designs. Or choose wallpaper murals. You can even paint your own "special effects."

Rough-hewn impact

A wood ceiling overhead—whether left natural, stained, or painted—infuses any room with welcome warmth and coziness that suits virtually any decorating style.

Round pine beams called *vigas* lend special, regional charm to the Santa Fe home pictured *at right*. The rough beams and flat pine planks, called *latillas,* play off beautifully against textured adobe walls and icy-smooth tile floors. A skylight keeps the feeling light and airy.

Although exposed wood ceilings often are created when a home is built, you can add beams, install one of the newer wood-patterned ceiling tiles, or nail up wood planks or grooved cedar plywood later.

FLOORS

More than any other background surface at home, we demand a lot of our floors. Not only do we expect them to withstand daily traffic and tracked-in grime, but we also insist that they *look* beautiful. That's asking a lot—but not the impossible, as long as you select your flooring carefully. Carpet is a common choice underfoot, but by no means the only one. Let's consider other options for backgrounds meant to be walked on.

Wood floors can take a lot of punishment and simply may be refinished every decade or so to keep them beautiful. Today's newest wood floors and sealers simplify upkeep, too. Just vacuum and dust-mop regularly, and wax occasionally.

You'll find lots of wood-floor options today. You can buy prefinished wood planks in a variety of styles, have unfinished wood floors installed and finished on site, or opt for an expensive (but almost maintenance-free) acrylic-impregnated wood floor. The latter has a special finish that goes right through the entire plank, meaning that even scratches are virtually invisible.

You can choose from an almost unlimited range of finishes, too, from dark stains to bleached or pickled floors. The pickled floor shown *opposite* is both airy and sophisticated. To create this effect, brush white paint or stain onto one small area of floor at a time; wipe the pigment off quickly for a soft, whitewashed effect.

Tiles—hard and soft

Hard-surface tile is another practical and beautiful flooring choice. Impervious to tracked-in dirt and moisture, it also creates a backdrop that's perfect for casual, country, or contemporary furnishings.

In the addition to an old house pictured *above*, quarry tile sets an earth-tone stage for pine furniture and country

accessories. A handwoven dhurrie rug brightens and helps define the conversation area.

If this kind of tile floor appeals to you but you want something softer underfoot, consider solid vinyl tiles that look surprisingly like natural materials. These tiles—in patterns that resemble brick, quarry tile, or slate—are warmer to the touch than their real counterparts and offer excellent wear-resistance. Although some solid vinyl tiles require professional installation, you can save money by installing peel-and-stick tiles yourself.

continued

Second in size only to wall area, floors have a major impact on the mood of your rooms. With the right background, you even can go so far as to suggest an indoor climate, no matter what the weather is outside. Both of the rooms shown here are in homes in cold regions, but their floors demonstrate very different approaches to creating winter retreats.

In the den pictured *at right,* sisal carpet helps those sitting there imagine the coming of spring or a trip to the tropics. Combined with the sisal carpet, a bamboo-base table, wicker armchairs, and a white cotton sofa further the airy, gardenlike scheme.

Nubby, woven sisal is a natural for dens, but is equally at home in living rooms, porches, and playrooms. Durable—and with an appealing, strawlike feel—sisal carpet can be installed wall to wall as shown here, or used as an area rug over carpeted, wood, tile, or sheet vinyl floors.

Thanks to a seamless envelope of commercial-grade, level-loop carpet that not only covers the floor but also sheathes the built-in banquettes and adjacent walls, the den shown *above* is as welcoming as a warm blanket, and as quiet as a snow-covered street. Matching gray-painted woodwork and shelves reinforce the cozy atmosphere.

70

WINDOWS

Walls, ceilings, and floors constitute the biggest background surfaces in any decorating scheme, but what you do with windows plays a vital role, too. Whether you want to emphasize a great view, play up fine old window moldings, or put your windows way in the background, you'll find a wide range of window dressings in all price ranges. On the next four pages, we'll show you some particularly handsome window treatments and discuss how to select the ones that are right for your windows.

I f you're fortunate enough to have beautiful windows, play them up. For example, classic tie-back draperies call attention to the gracious French doors shown *above.* Mounted at the ceiling line, the draperies emphasize the doors' height and frame a verdant view with soft folds of fabric.

Tiebacks work well with doors or windows that swing outward like these. If you want a softly romantic look but your doors open inward, use draperies or curtains that will clear the doors when they open, or shirr fabric panels onto sash rods mounted directly on each door. If privacy isn't a concern, consider framing your French doors with an elegant fabric swag.

If pleated shades, Roman shades, or mini-slat blinds are more your style, install them separately on each door, or mount them on the wall above the doors.

Blinds and shades

Window blinds and shades are always in style. Their very simplicity is a distinctive design statement. Clean-lined blind or shade treatments also can meld your windows into the background—a real plus in small spaces and where you want to emphasize other elements.

In the dining room shown *at right,* for example, plain mini-slat blinds are mounted inside the window casing to play up the home's nice old woodwork and provide an important contemporary element in the room's eclectic decorating scheme. The blinds, color-keyed to the off-white window trim, let in lots of light and air, yet screen the view of the house next door.

(continued)

A bay window deserves special treatment, and fortunately, there are lots to choose among. Shutters, whether traditional louvered panels or the wide-vane plantation shutters shown *above,* can be custom-cut to fit any bay or bow window. When painted white, as the ones in this living room are, shutters will create a luminous background for your furnishings.

As the photograph shows, you can use shutters with floor-to-ceiling glass, as well as with ordinary windows. You also might give a conventional picture window a modern, window-wall look by mounting shutters from floor to ceiling and perhaps adding a panel or two at either side of the window trim.

Prehinged shutter sets, available through large mail order catalogs, make installing shutters easier than ever. You also can make your own solid shutters by covering wood or plywood panels with fabric, wallpaper, or paint.

Other window strategies
If you want your windows to have a simple, light-filled look, consider vertical or mini-slat blinds, breezy curtains of sheer fabric, or today's newest pleated shades, which pull up, Roman-shade-style, into crisp accordion folds. You can

choose from opaque or semi-sheer fabric. To minimize heat gain, opt for an aluminized, reflective backing.

The fabrics you choose can dramatically alter the decorative mood of a window treatment. A Roman shade made of unbleached muslin, for instance, would have a casual, down-to-earth look; a bold graphic print would give the shade contemporary punch; and dressy fabrics would lend formal elegance.

In the photo *at right,* gauzy white organza lends a romantic air to Roman shades. The fabric softly filters sunlight without completely blocking either light or the view.

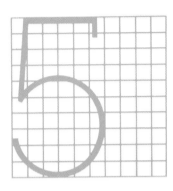

TRIED-AND-TRUE TECHNIQUES

You may know in your mind's eye what you want your house—or a particular room—to look like, but turning this vision into reality often is easier said than done. Usually the difficulty lies in not feeling certain about where and how to begin. Fortunately, there are any number of excellent and reliable techniques for getting a decorating scheme off the ground. In this chapter, we'll show you what some of them are.

RENEW A ROOM WITH FABRIC

Few of us start a decorating scheme completely from scratch. More often than not, what we seek is a spruce-up of an existing scheme, not a total—and costly—redo. If you have a room that's looking the worse for wear and you want to give it a lift, one of the quickest cures you can count on is to renew with fabric.

The living room pictured here was revived with an infusion of new upholstery fabric on the sofas and other seating pieces. An English floral chintz is the major scene setter. Used on the sofa, wing chair, and upholstered armchair, the delightful garden print is a colorful, eye-catching presence in this gracious, traditional setting. To avoid one-pattern monotony, the small love seat in the tête-à-tête grouping is covered in a solid blue-on-blue fabric that echoes a hue from the floral print.

A pale blue ceiling ties the scheme together and provides a sophisticated touch for the colonial-inspired setting. Other bits of blue are repeated in the soft, rich tones of the Oriental area rug, in the needlepoint chair cushion, and in accessories placed throughout the room.

If you decide that a fabric update is what your room needs, keep in mind that selecting patterns and prints is no longer the confusing task it used to be. Today, many companies offer a wide selection of coordinated fabrics, wall coverings, window treatments, and even floor coverings in virtually every style and color imaginable. All you need do is select the pattern or print you like best; the rest of the matching process already has been done for you.

USE COLOR COURAGEOUSLY

Of all the decorating tools at our disposal, color is our greatest ally. And when it's paint we call upon, there's no end to the rainbow of possibilities. The problem is, most of us are color shy. We may be tempted to try a new paint scheme, but we often fall back on no-risk colors—white, off-white, and beige. Breaking out of a play-it-safe syndrome takes a little extra planning and effort, but the results are well worth it.

A sense of drama is guaranteed when you paint a room a strong, imposing color such as brown, charcoal, or granite blue. In the living room pictured *above*, rich chocolate brown walls provide a warm and enveloping background for a miscellany of country and contemporary furnishings. Included in the mixture of styles are a modern velvet-covered sofa, a nineteenth-century half-spindle settee, an assortment of ladder-back chairs, and an old drum now put to use as a coffee table.

To keep this powerful hue from overwhelming the room, the ceiling, woodwork, and windows are punctuated in white. Additional color relief comes from the eye-catching Indian area rug, the toss pillows and seat cushions, and numerous accessories.

Dark colors aren't the only hues that make their presence known. Even the most delicate pastels, when used generously, can make a strong and memorable style statement. The bedroom shown *at right*, for example, gets its color punch from melon-color walls offset by a seafoam green carpet and a multicolor rag rug. For an extra measure of eye appeal, there's a four-poster dressed in a pleasing array of patterns and prints in pinks, reds, yellow, and orange. Note that the contemporary pine bed frame is painted to blend in with the walls.

USE A NEUTRAL PLUS ONE COLOR

Some of the most appealing room schemes are the easiest to pull together. One case in point is a neutral-plus-one-color combination. All you need to do is pick your favorite color and put it in company with a neutral choice. Whites, grays, browns, beiges, and taupes—and a spectrum of shades between—are among the most popular "un-colors." And of all the go-with-everything neutrals, white is the easiest to work with. There's not a color in the rainbow that clashes with white, so any combination you choose is sure to be a success.

The quiet, unaggressive qualities of neutral colors make them excellent choices for small rooms like the living area pictured here. Unlike bright, bold colors, which tend to advance toward the eye, neutrals are content to blend into the background, making small spaces seem larger than they really are.

Color comes from accents
This neutral-plus-one-color scheme combines beiges and whites with elegant burgundy accents. The burgundy, though used sparingly, is a major decorative influence in the understated setting. At the windows, for instance, the presence of dark red Roman shades draws attention to the beauty of the antique moldings that have been added to the plain window frames. To give them additional architectural interest, the moldings are painted a slightly darker shade than the walls. On the sofa and chairs, burgundy velvet toss pillows stand out in eye-catching contrast to the white all-wool upholstery.

Variety is essential
Notice that care has been taken to balance light, medium, and dark color values around the room. Without this kind of variety, a neutral color scheme is apt to look bland.

Also important in a neutral scheme is the presence of pattern and texture. Here pattern variety comes from an Oriental area rug and the upholstery fabric on a pair of pull-up stools. The juxtaposition of sleek and shiny accessories against the soft and nubby fabrics and floor coverings offers a nice interplay of textures.

STAY WITH A SINGLE COLOR FAMILY

Another way to take advantage of neutrals is to concentrate on variations of a single shade. With this approach, you select a neutral such as gray or brown, then use it in multiple ways. Done right, the look is visually soothing and highly sophisticated. Done wrong, however, a monochromatic or one-color-family scheme can look bland and dull. The best way to keep blandness at bay is to plan for a variety of textures, patterns, furniture shapes, and lighting effects.

Gray, in a range of shades from deep to delicate, assumes a major role in the high-style, eclectically furnished living room pictured *at right.*

The soothing scheme gets its start on the walls. Although they look painted, the wall surfaces actually are upholstered in a suedelike fabric that's gray with a hint of khaki. A similarly soft-textured one-color effect could be achieved with a wallpaper or vinyl wall covering designed to simulate the look of fabric. White-painted woodwork and trim serve as a decorative punctuation mark and keep the gray background from making the scheme too subdued.

The furnishings themselves represent a mélange of styles, but in the context of an all-neutral scheme, their coloring serves as a common denominator. Included in the mix is a loose-cushion contemporary sofa covered in white wool, two French *bergère* chairs, a black-lacquered Oriental-style coffee table, and a small Oriental tray table.

A distinctive black and white geometric area rug anchors the grouping. Although the rug's pattern is decidedly different in scale and mood from the mini-print covering the armchairs, the two patterns coexist beautifully. The clue to their compatibility lies in their common color ground and the difference in their size and scale, which is distinct enough to keep them from battling with each other.

AIM FOR THE RIGHT ROOM ARRANGEMENT

In the final analysis, it's not the furniture, the color scheme, or the choice of art and accessories that makes a room look good and function well. Nor is it the size or the shape of the space. What really matters more than anything else is how you arrange a room for comfort, flexibility, and convenience. This may sound simple enough, but all too often, room arrangement is treated as an afterthought. And when this happens, it's the people who use the room who get short-changed.

Though it's small, narrow, and lacking in architectural interest, the tract-house living/dining area shown *at right* looks great and functions beautifully because of its well-conceived furniture arrangement.

Rather than try to cram standard-size, space-eating furniture into this room, the owners chose flexible, re-arrangeable modular seating pieces to create a congenial conversation grouping. Even though the house lacks a separate dining room, they were able to create the semblance of one by placing the love seats face-to-face and well away from the wall. Adding to the sense of two separate rooms is the placement of the cotton dhurrie area rug. It not only visually and decoratively defines the seating area, but also serves as a colorful demarcation of the living and dining ends of the room.

As is often the case in recent-vintage tract houses, this home lacks a natural focal point such as a fireplace. To create a substitute center of interest here, the owners stacked see-through storage cubes in front of the tall, narrow window, then filled the slots with plants and accessory items. Framed posters provide additional eye-catching impact.

The dining "room" has its own focal point in the form of a small-scale pine hutch. Other furnishings include an expandable gate-leg pine table and four chrome-and-cane Cesca chairs. On the wall facing the hutch (not shown) is a custom-made, wall-hung serving buffet with a glass ledge lighted from beneath. The large hanging lamp centered above the dining table provides a useful accent, too, further defining that part of the room as space with a separate function.

USE ONE FABRIC FOR ALL IT'S WORTH

Here's another way to make fabric your best decorating asset: Use a single smashing pattern or print to set the style of a room. Better still, whether used for window treatments, seat cushions, bed coverings, tablecloths, slipcovers, or for shirred or upholstered wall coverings, fabric gives you almost infinite variety at reasonable cost. In fact, fabric is usually an excellent buy.

The bedroom pictured *at right* owes much of its romance and charm to a delightful floral fabric and matching wall covering used with flair throughout the room. The garden-fresh treatment includes a gathered dust ruffle, flounced pillow shams, and simple white cotton curtains trimmed to match the fabric-covered plywood valance. Even the pleated shades topping the crystal lamp bases are part of the fabric act.

Floral fabrics, whether their patterns are as bold as that pictured here or on a daintier scale, seem to lend themselves to decorating motifs that evoke a simpler past. Here, that fabric is in perfect keeping with the cottagelike appeal of the delicately curved iron and brass bed, the antique nightstands, and the statuesque colonial-style highboy. The bed, though new, evokes a feeling of Victorian times.

Any pattern, of course, whether floral, abstract, or geometric, lends itself to interesting color use. For example, you might coordinate solid or reverse-pattern curtains and cushions with accent colors in the fabric. Or, you might paint walls, woodwork, and window trim to match one of the colors in the fabric print.

There's another advantage to decorating with fabric, beyond the aesthetic appeal that fabric-oriented rooms have. That not-so-secret factor is economics. Yard goods are available in all price ranges. Bed sheets, particularly when they're on sale, provide even more striking value, and have the added plus of coming in much wider widths than standard fabrics. If you happen to be handy with a sewing machine, the cost of decorating with fabric becomes even more affordable.

CALL ATTENTION TO STRUCTURAL DETAILS

If you're fortunate enough to live in a house with architectural assets, by all means play up their beautiful presence. Woodwork, plasterwork, moldings, wainscoting, dados, cornices, window trim, door and wall panels, fireplaces, and other architectural details are decorative elements in their own right. Properly accentuated with paint, stain, or contrasting walls, they add character to any room. Take a look around your house to see if there are structural elements that deserve to be emphasized.

In the gracious living room pictured here, the architecture has been emphasized with paint, in colors carefully selected to bring out the best of the room's style. The woodwork and the frames of the tall windows are a rich shade of blue-gray, which makes these features stand out with dramatic flair against the walls. Painted a paler shade of the same color, the walls create a subtle backdrop for the furnishings. By leaving the windows unadorned except by paint, the homeowners have given these striking architectural elements the attention they deserve.

The room's furnishings are a blend of simple shapes and subtle but far-from-dull colors. A polished-cotton sofa is covered in a deep version of the room's blue-gray theme color. Two Haitian cotton chairs and a mirror-finish coffee table provide textural contrast and color variety, without distracting the eye from the room itself. The black marble fireplace, as shiny as the table, is another of the room's architectural beauties.

Create your own architecture

If you live in a house that lacks interesting architectural details, consider adding your own. Many hardware stores and building supply outlets sell easy-to-install reproduction moldings, chair rails, and other architectural elements that look much like those found in period homes.

Also widely available are wall-covering borders that have the look of woodwork, paneling, moldings, and ornate plaster relief decorations. You also can use materials such as paint, ribbon, adhesive tape, or fabric to create distinctive "architectural" effects.

STRIP DOWN YOUR DECORATING

The pared-down look stands on its own as an elegant approach to interior design. With this kind of scheme, it's the quality of the furnishings and decoration, not their quantity, that makes a room memorable. The "less is more" look is deceptively simple. In a minimalist setting, there is very little to distract the eye. This emphasizes each and every object. With stripped-down decorating, great care must be taken to select furniture, artwork, and accessories that are truly worthy of attention.

Totally devoid of frills and furbelows, this sophisticated master bedroom defies convention in a number of exciting ways. Traditional bedroom accoutrements—nightstands, dressing tables, and large chests of drawers—are notably absent from the high-style scheme. In place of a more conventional scheme is a pared-down look that is simple, understated, and serene.

A single gray-green background color wraps the room in a quiet cocoon of color. The wall-to-wall carpet is the flat-weave commercial variety often found in office buildings and other public places, emphasizing the room's unfettered, no-nonsense appeal.

The wall behind the bed is covered with mini-slat blinds in the same gray-green color as the other walls and floor. The treatment extends from floor to ceiling and covers not only the window but also the solid wall next to it. At night, when the blinds are shut, the window treatment turns into an unbroken shiny metal surface.

What keeps this stripped-down scheme from looking stark and sterile is the artwork. A series of colorful contemporary prints, hung low for dramatic effect, serves as bright counterpoint for the quiet scheme. The effect is heightened by the single-file arrangement and the wide white mats, which help separate the prints from the dark wall.

The bed is simply a mattress placed atop a box spring that rests directly on the floor. The bed backs up to a custom-made plastic-laminate-covered dresser that doubles as a headboard. Attached to the top of the headboard/dresser are two sleek, swing-arm reading lamps—appropriate choices for the simple setting.

STRIVE FOR PERSONAL STYLE

Dull rooms, like dull people, often are deficient in spirit and style. In a humdrum setting, the furniture may well be the finest, and the arrangement just right, but if the essential ingredient—personality—is missing, then all is for naught. How does one avoid decorative boredom? The best way is to instill a sense of yourself in the room. This can easily be accomplished by infusing it with your favorite things—artwork, hobbies and handiwork, and accessories.

Nearly anything goes when it comes to personalizing a room. What matters most is that the objects on display have meaning to you. In other words, try to be selective with what you display. Accessories, no matter what they are or how much they cost, are more likely to be appreciated—by you and others—when they reflect your particular tastes and interests.

Personal style abounds in the living room pictured here. Though the furnishings, artwork, and accessories represent a variety of periods and styles, the separate pieces are all completely compatible. Contemporary and antique furnishings keep beautiful company with a just-for-fun collection of antique toys, American folk art, colorful prints, baskets, and one-of-a-kind contemporary sculpture.

Many of the homeowner's prized possessions were serendipitous finds at flea markets, garage sales, and country auctions. The smaller collectibles and favorite books are showcased in built-in shelves that wrap around a recessed window. The room's *pièce de résistance,* a wooden ballerina-and-horse sculpture, is prominently displayed atop an old library table.

A neutral color scheme was chosen for the room to avoid competing with the art and accessories. Walls and woodwork are painted eggshell white, and the seating pieces—two love seats and a sofa—are upholstered in tailored soft gray flannel. The U-shape arrangement encourages conversation, and provides several ideal vantage points for admiring the room's many items of interest.

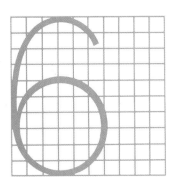

FINDING WHAT YOU NEED

Considering the abundance of furnishings and accessories in the marketplace today, you may sometimes wonder where to shop for the best buys. Where you shop, of course, depends on the sort of furnishings you need and what you can afford to pay for them. This chapter explores the wealth of sources from which to choose and discusses what you can expect from each.

DEPARTMENT STORES, HOME STORES, AND SPECIALTY SHOPS

Of all the many sources of home furnishings consumers throughout the country can turn to, three types of retail stores are perhaps the best-known:
• *Department stores* with many home-oriented areas.
• *Home stores*—department stores devoted solely to furnishings, housewares, and accessories.
• *Specialty shops* that concentrate on one type or style of item, such as wall coverings, window treatments, or Scandinavian furniture.

The type of store you shop in depends in part on what's available in your area and in part on how much time and money you have to spend. The scale of the project you have in mind is also an important factor. If, for example, you're in the market for a living room lamp, you may be better off to confine your shopping to lighting stores. On the other hand, if you want to completely refurbish a room or two, you might be better off to visit a large "home" or department store where you'll find a wide variety of goods.

Because of the variety they offer, department and "home" stores are the most popular sources of furnishings. When you're looking for carpet, window treatments, *and* some major furniture pieces, it's hard to beat a large store of that kind, especially if time is a factor. The home store frequently combines its decorative resources into attractive room settings and vignettes, like the one pictured *opposite,* which not only provide a selection of merchandise, but also offer decorating ideas.

You may find, however, that specialty shops offer the broadest selection of goods within a given category, so if you have the time and decorating know-how, you might want to do your shopping on an item-by-item basis.

Money matters
You'll get a lot more mileage from your shopping dollar if you spend the most on what has to last the longest and is likely to get the hardest wear. For instance, if your budget is tight, invest in good hall carpet and cut back on the quality of the bedroom floor covering. Similarly, spend money on a good sofa, even if it means making do with an improvised coffee table for awhile.

In the long run, you'll find that buying a few good pieces over a period of time is a wiser investment than filling an entire space with items that are poorly made or of mediocre design. One special piece of furniture, an elegant area rug, or a piece of original art can set the mood for an entire room and—more important— give you pleasure for years to come.

Another way to make the most of your furnishings budget is to plan ahead. Because the furnishings business is a seasonal one, you can save as much as 50 percent if you buy off-season. Furniture sales usually take place after Christmas and again in July and August when business is slow and stores are preparing for manufacturers' new lines.

Above all, remember that the best buys are those that offer good value. Look for pieces that are flexible, functional, and durable as well as attractive and comfortable.

CATALOG SHOPPING

Today you can shop in some of the finest home furnishings stores in the country without venturing beyond your own door. Whether you're in the market for a roomful of furniture or just the perfect accessory, you may well be able to find precisely what you have in mind simply by thumbing through catalogs. You can order by phone or by mail and be certain of prompt delivery, careful packaging, and top-quality merchandise. Plain or fancy, functional or fun, you can get whatever you need without ever leaving home.

Poring over a giant mail-order catalog used to be an evening's entertainment—a time for armchair window shopping and fantasizing. Catalogs still give you a window on the world, and you'll find they offer more today than ever before. Better yet, mail-order companies are in hot competition with one another to sell top-quality merchandise at prices that appeal to consumers.

A burgeoning market
The catalog market, once dominated by such mail-order giants as Spiegel, Sears, J.C. Penney, and Montgomery Ward, has expanded tremendously in the past several years. A vast number of specialty companies have joined the marketplace, and now you can purchase everything from inventive kitchen gadgets to exquisite handmade linens through an intriguing collection of catalogs.

The broad range of goods available through these catalogs—the items pictured *opposite* are just a sampling—makes shopping from them highly appealing, even for those who live in cities where large selections of merchandise are available. For those who don't live in large metropolitan areas, catalog shopping offers even more advantages, allowing people everywhere to purchase just about everything available to city dwellers.

Placing your order
Ordering from a catalog can save you time and sometimes money, but because you can't examine the goods firsthand, it's important to keep several pointers in mind as you complete your order.

• Make it a policy to buy from companies with established reputations. If you're not familiar with a firm, check with the Better Business Bureau or local consumer protection office.
• Before ordering, read the product description carefully for pertinent information. Don't rely on a photograph.
• Some catalogs state that a comparable substitute will be sent if what you ordered is not available. If you don't want a substitute, clearly say so.
• Before you buy, find out whether the merchandise you want is offered on a "satisfaction-guaranteed" or "money-back" basis. If the company's refund policy is unclear, ask for clarification.
• Check warranty terms, especially if you're purchasing major items. Find out what recourse you have if the product doesn't live up to the manufacturer's specifications. Determine also who pays postage or shipping charges for returned items.

If you plan to pay in installments, study the credit plan to find out exactly how much you will pay and when.
• Keep a record of your order, including the name and address of the company and the date you placed the order. Also, make note of the delivery date for your order.
• Don't send cash through the mail; instead, send a personal check, money order, or major credit card number. Be certain to include shipping and handling charges and applicable sales taxes.

Getting started
If you're new to the catalog marketplace, the following list will help you acquire a basic supply of good catalogs. All of the companies are well-established firms with reputations for merchandising top-quality home furnishings. Since mail-order marketers often exchange mailing lists, you may find yourself receiving many catalogs after you've sent away for a few. Bear in mind, too, that some companies charge for their catalogs; the fee is often credited to your first purchase.

Adam York
340 Poplar St.
Hanover, PA 17331
Conran's
145 Huguenot St.
New Rochelle, NY 10801
Crate and Barrel
190 Northfield Rd.
Northfield, IL 60093
Fabrications
146 E. 56th St.
New York, NY 10022
Fran's Basket House
Rte. 10
Succasunna, NJ 07876
George Kovacs
831 Madison Ave.
New York, NY 10021
Hammacher Schlemmer
147 E. 57th St.
New York, NY 10022
The Horchow Collection
P.O. Box 34257
Dallas, TX 75234
J.C. Penney Co., Inc.
Box 2056
Milwaukee, WI 53201
Montgomery Ward
Chicago, IL 60607
Sears, Roebuck and Co.
Sears Tower
Chicago, IL 60684
Spiegel
1061 W. 35th St.
Chicago, IL 60609
Williams-Sonoma
Box 3792
San Francisco, CA 94119

ANTIQUES SHOPS AND AUCTIONS

A link with the past, a respect for handcraftsmanship, the individuality of one-of-a-kind pieces, investment—these are only some of the reasons for buying antiques. No matter what motivates you to acquire antiques for your home, you'd be wise to assimilate some background information before you go off, cash in hand, into the unpredictable world of antiques shops and auctions.

Estate sales, auctions, and stores that specialize in antiques are the best places to look for vintage finds. You might come across a particularly good piece at a flea market or garage sale, but the chances are relatively slim.

Auctions

Auctions constitute some of the best sources of antiques in the marketplace. Because such a variety of items crosses the auction block, auctions are great places to learn about antiques and collectibles. They are also good places to uncover bargains, since items generally sell at auction for about half what they sell for at retail.

An important point to bear in mind if you intend to buy at auction is that you should never bid on a piece you haven't examined. Most auction houses publish catalogs in advance of a sale that describe the pieces to be sold and estimate their value. If you see anything in the catalog that interests you, make a point of looking it over carefully prior to the sale. Pieces to be sold will always be exhibited beforehand. The exhibition may take place a few days or a few hours before the auction, but you should examine each item you're considering placing a bid on so you'll know if it is in good condition and is accurately described in the catalog.

If you've never bought at auction before, arrive at the salesroom in plenty of time to get a seat within clear view of the auctioneer. You'll be certain to be seen and can concentrate on your bidding. Be sure you've determined the increments or dollar increases that will be applied during bidding. The increments may be $25, $50, $100, or even $1,000 or more depending on the items' estimated values

and price levels reached during bidding. If you don't understand how the increments will change, ask the auctioneer to explain the scale to you. This is information you must understand if you're to know how much you've raised the price when you signal a bid.

Contrary to what many people assume, bidding is not a complex process. Although bidding may proceed rapidly enough during some auctions to confuse or unnerve an amateur, the procedure is a very simple one. Bidding is opened by the auctioneer, who acknowledges bids from the audience until no further bids are offered. Usually a raised hand, catalog, or numbered paddle signals a bid.

The best way to learn the ins and outs of buying at auction is to explore auction houses and attend as many of their sales as you can. Even if you don't participate, you can learn by observing.

Antiques dealers

A dealer may be your best source if you're searching for rare items. Ask fellow collectors or local appraisers for recommendations. To avoid costly mistakes, do your research before you buy. When you're ready to make a purchase, don't hesitate to negotiate the price. Ask for an itemized receipt that describes the piece and provides written proof of authenticity. An antique is currently defined as any item at least 100 years old. However, remember that not all antiques are fine antiques and that there are a number of factors besides age that determine the value of a piece.

Although shops that specialize in antiques are generally the best sources for buying antiques at retail, a growing number of department stores

are incorporating antiques boutiques like the one pictured here. It's unlikely you'll find a wide variety of pieces in such boutiques, but those you do see are likely to be good quality and somewhat unusual.

Assessing value

When shopping the antiques circuit, it doesn't take long before you realize that the prices of antique furnishings vary greatly. Some of the disparity comes from the dealers involved, but other differences reflect the furniture's features. Here is a list of things that can influence price.

• *Condition.* Naturally a piece in mint condition will command a higher price than one that is falling apart.

• *Materials.* Some antiques, especially fine wood furnishings, soar to the top of the price scale. Accent materials such as brass or silver hardware and leaded or beveled glass also increase value—and cost.

• *Authenticity, source, and origin.* When a piece is signed or dated, or its age, manufacturer, or ownership are documented in some other way, expect to pay for the pedigree. If the piece was made by a famous craftsman, the price is likely to be even higher.

• *Availability.* The scarcer an item is, the more it's likely to be sought after—and the more expensive it's likely to be.

FINDING WHAT YOU NEED

DESIGN COLLECTIONS

One of the easiest ways to put together a great-looking room scheme is to use a prematched design collection. Coordinated collections assembled by designers, manufacturers, and even some retail outlets often include fabrics, wall coverings, rugs, paint, bed and table linens, and a wide variety of decorative accessories. No matter what your favorite decorating style, you'll find collections designed to suit both your budget and your taste.

Collections help a do-it-yourself decorator produce gratifying results quickly and easily. You simply decide on the decorating style you prefer, then select a design collection for your room that incorporates elements in that style.

Basically, collections do three things: They provide coordinated merchandise in a particular style; they offer pre-planned color coordination; and they provide a selection of patterns that are designed to work together. In short, collections provide imaginative and failure-free ways to combine colors, mix and match patterns, and lend professional flair to a design scheme. These premixed materials take the guesswork out of selecting compatible patterns and can help turn a pattern-shy amateur into a pattern-sure decorator practically overnight.

What's available
Design collections run the gamut from the simple, which often include companion wallpaper and fabrics only, to the elaborate, which offer almost every type of home furnishing imaginable, from flatware to lampshades. All are designed to simplify the task of decorating your home.

You may already be familiar with such collections as *Gear, Marimekko, Pierre Deux,* and *Laura Ashley.* Recently, increasing numbers of designers have entered the field, widening the range of offerings.

The room pictured here is decorated almost entirely with fabrics and accessories from a single designer collection; the furniture is from other sources. The vibrant, contemporary decorative accessories featured here are available at department stores throughout the country. Other collections are marketed by chains of retail boutiques, as well as through mail-order catalogs.

Mixing and matching
Just about every decorating style, from country to contemporary, is represented in design collections, but usually each collection is distinguished by only one style.

Generally, several patterns are available within a collection and those patterns come in four or five different colors—or colorways as they are sometimes called. This makes it easy to choose a color scheme: You merely pick the color you like and then combine solids and patterns from that color family. Because items in the entire collection have probably been designed to work together, you can also choose accents from another color family in the same collection and be sure ahead of time that they're compatible.

You may want to combine more than one pattern in a room. Using a design collection, you can mix and match with confidence. That's because most offer a selection of coordinated patterns—stripes, florals, and mini-prints, for example—that are all designed to work together.

Creating your own collection
Once you've become familiar with how design collections make combinations work, you may feel confident enough in your own abilities to put together your own personal "collection." Generally speaking, strong patterns work best when given top billing. A large-scale floral will work well with a medium-scale geometric pattern and a mini-print. Small-scale patterns can add punch to a room without vying for attention with the dominant patterns, because small-scale patterns often appear to be solid colors when viewed from a distance.

Finding a common color theme is one of the best ways to tie two or more patterns together. And just as patterns can be brought together with the use of color, pattern can also help you create a color scheme. One almost fail-safe method is to take your color scheme from a fabric pattern that you're using in a room. A common technique is to choose a paler tint for larger areas, such as the walls, ceiling, and possibly the floor. Then take a brighter color from the pattern for, say, major upholstered pieces, or draperies, or the floor covering. It's usually best to consider reserving the boldest or brightest colors for accents—pillows, area rugs, and other accessories. This is only one approach, of course: If you'd like to be a bit more adventurous, you can create exciting schemes by varying this format and using stronger colors for larger areas.

Another color tip to remember: You'll have a more cohesive and successful scheme if you don't give two or more colors equal importance in a room. Give one dominance, and let the other play counterpoint. And think twice about using a color just once—if you bring in a yellow throw pillow, you may want to add corresponding yellow touches elsewhere in the room.

FINDING WHAT YOU NEED

ALTERNATIVE SOURCES

If your tastes are somewhat eclectic, your budget a little tight, or your spirit a bit adventurous, you may be interested in exploring alternative sources for furnishings and accessories. Office furniture retailers, import outlets, architectural salvage companies, stores that specialize in unfinished furniture, and commercial display houses are all excellent and interesting alternative sources of home decorating items.

Successful shopping is a combination of know-how and imagination. Know-how is the ability to judge quality, single out the best values, and define personal tastes. Imagination is what gives your home individuality; it's also what helps you see the potential in furniture "buys" that other shoppers may overlook.

Home from the office

Office furniture, for example, can work very well in many room arrangements, yet the idea of using it never occurs to many people. Office furnishings have come a long way from the days of metal desks and filing cabinets. Today's offerings also include a broad selection of tables, seating, storage units, lamps, and accessories. Many of these pieces are available in a variety of finishes and fabrics. And at office supply stores you may find authentic design classics, such as Mies van der Rohe's Barcelona chair, that may not be available at department stores and other retail outlets.

The quality of commercial office furniture is often quite high because these pieces are meant to endure years of use. Prices may be high, too, however, and you may discover that some dealers are loath to bother with selling a single chair, for instance, because they are accustomed to writing up large orders.

Import shops

Many import shops carry not only small kitchen items and assorted gadgets but a good variety of well-designed furniture and larger accent pieces. Such outlets are excellent sources for rattan, bamboo, and wicker pieces like those shown here, as well as unusual brass items,

interesting ceramics and kitchenware, and inexpensive floor coverings.

Architectural salvage firms

Firms specializing in architectural salvage are great places to find unusual decorating items. There's a wide assortment of architectural items available at the salvage stores and warehouses that are proliferating throughout the country. The development of this new source of decorative items parallels the widespread and ever-growing interest in renovating and rehabilitating old buildings.

You can find practical objects ranging from mantelpieces to plumbing and lighting fixtures to bookcases—and much more. They're usually snapped up at a brisk rate by people who plan to use them not only to replace lost originals but also in innovative new ways as decorating elements.

Many architectural salvage firms also offer design and renovation advice and services, and will often search out specific items on request. Most dealers are also more than willing to suggest suitable uses for the items they sell.

Unfinished finds

If you still think of unfinished furniture as nothing but so-so styling and stapled-together construction, you're in for some nice surprises. Bargain-basement pieces still exist, but now you also can find well-made unfinished pieces in a wide variety of styles and woods. Whether your tastes run to standard traditional, contemporary, French, English, or Early American designs, you will have no difficulty locating pieces to suit you.

The construction methods and the kind of wood used for

unfinished furniture usually determine its price. Low-end pieces will be made of soft white pine, or have fiberboard bottoms and sides and nailed-together frames. Drawers will generally be held together with staples.

Moderate-price items are typically made of knotty pine. The most costly unfinished furniture is made of hardwoods such as maple, birch, and aspen; top-of-the-line pieces may be made of solid cherry, oak, or walnut.

Top-quality unfinished hardwood furniture, like its finished counterpart, most often features dovetailed construction and frames that have been blocked and glued. Sides, doors, and drawers will be made of wood, and drawers will have center guides. Doors will hang true on their hinges.

Display houses

You'd be surprised at the variety of furnishings and decorative accessories that can be acquired through display houses, which are commercial outlets that specialize in display pieces for the retail and theatrical trades. And because pieces carried by such outlets often have been used, you can frequently purchase them at bargain prices.

The only disadvantage to shopping display houses is that many of the items are one-of-a-kind, so you may not be able to assemble a complete collection of similar furniture. However, much of what display outlets offer for sale is imaginative in design, and it's worth the trip to see what's available. Also, the stock of such outlets changes frequently, so if you don't find anything suitable the first time around, it's quite possible you'll discover precisely what you need on subsequent visits.

PROFESSIONAL DESIGNERS AND DECORATORS

Hiring a professional interior designer can be the best decorating investment you make. A professional's expertise in planning room arrangements, coordinating colors and textures, and working within a budget can help you make wise decorating decisions and avoid costly mistakes. Because there are many different types of interior design services from which to choose, it's important to shop around for the one that will work best for you. Here are some guidelines to help you choose wisely.

Professional interior designers all perform similar work, but there are some subtle distinctions among the services they offer.

• An *independent designer* may work alone in his or her home, a small shop, or an office, or may be associated with a decorating firm. You can expect an independent designer to help you work out floor plans, coordinate color schemes, obtain fabric samples, and choose furniture—all within your budget. To simplify your furniture shopping, the designer will accompany or direct you to decorator showrooms, antiques shops, and other stores, or help you make selections from sample books.

• A *staff designer* working for a furniture or department store may use a similar approach. If the store has a decorating studio, like the one pictured *opposite,* it usually offers a wider selection of furnishings than you'd find in the retail departments of the store. Staff designers usually work for large stores or regional or national chains; some smaller furniture or department stores also advertise decorating services, but in most instances, you must choose from furniture and materials carried in the retail section of the store.

Finding the right designer

One of the best ways to find a reliable designer is through recommendations from friends and neighbors. Another good way is to visit decorators' showcase houses in your area; these usually feature the work of local designers. You also can learn a good deal about local talent simply by strolling through furniture or department stores. If you see model rooms that you find particularly appealing, ask who designed them.

When you've narrowed the field a bit, check the credentials and affiliations of the designers in whom you're interested. Membership in the American Society of Interior Designers (A.S.I.D.) is a good indication of a designer's competence because applicants must pass a stringent examination to qualify. Membership is voluntary, however, and many good designers don't belong to the organization. For a list of members in your area, write to the American Society of Interior Designers, 1430 Broadway, New York, NY 10018. Or look for A.S.I.D. members listed in the Yellow Pages of your city's phone book.

Keep in mind that openness is the key to working successfully with a professional designer. Be frank about how much money you can afford to spend. And be equally frank about your family's style preferences, favorite colors, and habits and hobbies. If you can't part with a favorite sofa, for instance, simply tell your designer to work it into the room scheme. After all, that's his or her job—to help you create a setting you will like and be comfortable in.

What does professional advice cost?

In some cases, hiring a professional designer doesn't cost you any more than buying furniture and materials on your own without help. Designers affiliated with department or furniture stores, for example, work on a percentage basis, which means they get a store commission on the merchandise they sell. Some stores require that you spend a minimum of $1,000 to $2,000 on furniture to receive complete decorating services, so it's wise to discuss store

requirements with the designer before you begin working with him or her.

Some independent designers also work on a percentage basis. They buy direct from their sources at wholesale prices, sell to their clients at retail (approximately one-third to one-half above wholesale price), and pocket the difference without charging an additional fee.

Most independent designers do charge consultation and design fees, however. Consultation rates generally range from $30 to $100 an hour and many designers require a two-hour minimum. An average fee for planning a room is $100. If extensive drafting of room schemes is necessary or samples of materials are presented, the fee may be higher. A charge of $500 a day will probably cover the drafting of a basic scheme for an entire house, a complete listing of furnishings outlets for the items specified, and all costs. A scheme for an average house could typically be developed in a single day, though design work for an unusually large home, or a complex plan, might take longer.

Billing methods may vary. If the designer works for a store where you have credit, you can simply charge the decorator's services to your account. Many independent designers draw up letters of agreement outlining the services to be performed and the payment schedule for those services. It's not uncommon to be asked for a deposit of up to 50 percent of the total estimated cost at the time work begins, with the balance due upon completion of the job. Some designers, though, charge for furnishings and services as they're delivered.

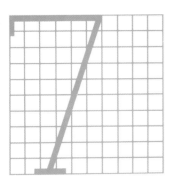

DECORATING CASE STUDIES

The way you approach a decorating project depends a great deal on your starting point. If you've just moved into your first house or apartment, then your needs and priorities will be quite different from those of someone who's lived in the same place for years, or who has accumulated a lifetime's worth of belongings. In this chapter, we'll show you five decorating schemes and tell you how each developed.

STARTING FROM SCRATCH

Even if you're a first-time homeowner or renter, it's not likely that you're beginning your decorating scheme entirely from scratch. Chances are, you've been heir to hand-me-downs from family or friends. But the day will come, if it hasn't already, that you'll want to personalize your surroundings with your own acquisitions. Our main words-to-the-wise at this point are these: Take your time. Even if you can afford it, avoid the temptation to buy a roomful or houseful of furniture all at once. The most successful decorating schemes are those that evolve slowly over a period of time.

Our first case study is that of a California woman who decorated her 35-year-old ranch on a limited budget. Her dining room, pictured *at right,* though still in the making, is nevertheless a delight. An old metal porch table, lavishly skirted with two cloths sewn from sheets, rests atop a dhurrie rug bought on sale. Seating is provided by classic canvas-seat director's chairs that have been customized with hand-made cushions. Artwork consists of colorful posters. Although the room is furnished with interim pieces, there's nothing makeshift about it.

(continued)

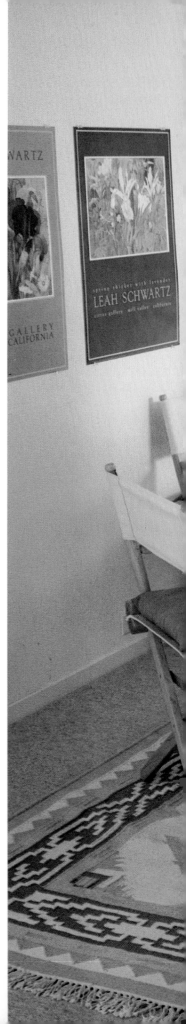

STARTING FROM SCRATCH
(continued)

From the dining room shown on the preceding pages, you look into the living room pictured *at right*. Here modular seating pieces make excellent choices for the owner's starting-out scheme. They're a snap to rearrange in any configuration, and thus can adapt easily to changing living needs.

Other flexible furnishings include the woven-wicker trunk—used here as an end table—and a small white cube. The trunk offers the bonus of hidden storage, and the plastic-laminate cube is easy to position wherever and whenever an extra table is needed.

As you can see, the same pink, blue, and white color combination found in the dining room is repeated here. What's more, an entirely new scheme could be created simply by changing the artwork, the area rug, and the fabric on the toss pillows.

Starting from scratch in the master bedroom, shown *above*, meant calling on modulars to create much-needed storage space. Although the combination wall unit/window seat looks like a costly built-in, it's not. The white-lacquered storage pieces are knock-downs that come with optional doors, drawers, and shelves. The homeowner customized her own wall system by picking and choosing from the options available, then assembling the components to suit her space and storage needs. Tall bookcases frame the window, and matching chests provide a double-duty storage/seating ledge that's topped with plump cushions for lounging.

A NEW LOOK ON A BUDGET

There's no reason why a limited budget should put a damper on your decorating dreams. These days, you can easily create an eye-pleasing environment without going to great expense or sacrificing on looks or quality. By developing an eye for well-designed, well-made furnishings, you'll find that your decorating dollars can stretch a surprisingly long way.

Located in an old school, pictured *above,* that's been converted to condominiums, the small living-room-plus-sleeping-loft apartment featured here and on the next two pages is home to a young single person. The furnishings in this well-planned 767-square-foot space are simple, tasteful, and functional, too.

The sunny yellow walls provide a warm welcome. They're highlighted by the contrasting dark blue of the partial wall behind the spiral staircase, the navy blue love seat, and two bright green armless chairs.

The upholstered pieces—all inexpensive, foam-filled items—provide comfortable seating by day. For overnight guests, the convertible units are flipped out to provide sleeping space for four.

Casually arranged cushions add visual interest and pick up the green of the chairs. White wire shelf units, a sisal rug, and a glass-topped coffee table are low in cost but high in style. *(continued)*

A NEW LOOK ON A BUDGET
(continued)

Although the classroom-turned-condo is small, it has a spacious air. Because most rooms in the building originally had 14-foot-high ceilings, they were naturals for vertically subdividing with lofts. The sleeping loft/study, pictured *at right,* offers ample headroom and provides a bird's-eye view of the living room below.

Thanks to the use of small-scale, multiuse furnishings, the loft functions beautifully in its dual roles. A platform bed, topped with colorful toss pillows, becomes a sofa by day; a drafting table turns into a flat-surface desk when needed. A white-lacquered chest of drawers also does double duty as a storage spot for clothes and office supplies. Although the loft has no windows, a newly installed skylight floods the room with daylight.

An open spiral staircase, shown *above,* provides easy access to the aerie. Nestled at the foot of the stairs is a cozy dining nook. The metal café table and the sleek, stackable chairs, designed for both indoor and outdoor use, are contemporary classics. Placed against the brilliant blue-painted wall, the inexpensive table and chairs are economy-size standouts.

IMPROVING ON WHAT YOU HAVE

As we've already mentioned, decorating often is not so much a matter of starting from scratch but of improving on what you already have. Even the most beautifully furnished rooms eventually look the worse for wear, and all rooms stand to benefit from an occasional spruce-up. If your present scheme has seen better days, maybe you need to change only a few elements for a transformation like the one shown here.

Although it started out with a ho-hum decorating scheme (see the "before" inset photo *opposite*), the apartment living room pictured *at right* and *above* now exudes high style.

The owner, who is rarely home during the day, asked an interior designer to create a cozy nighttime milieu. Without purchasing any new furniture, the designer fulfilled the request. The only new elements, in addition to a dramatic dark gray paint job, were the vertical blinds, a pleated shade, a colorful dhurrie rug, and a linenlike fabric used to re-cover the sofa. Black cube tables and the old dining table now serving as a desk in the solarium were brought in from other rooms. The original mustard-color carpet was removed to expose a terrazzo floor beneath. *(continued)*

IMPROVING ON WHAT YOU HAVE
(continued)

Any room, no matter how it's furnished, always can be improved with a fresh coat of paint. And when it's a bold or bright color you call upon, there's no end to the rainbow of improvements you can make.

In the small bedroom pictured *at left,* paint performs its decorative magic in several pleasing ways. White paint gives new life to the old iron-and-brass bed, and a rich blue-green on the walls enlivens the entire room. Because the windows are worthy of extra attention, their tall arched frames have been emphasized with several coats of white semigloss paint. The boudoir chair in the foreground, a long-time household possession, is perked up with a slipcover in a diminutive country print.

It's the paint again that deserves most of the credit for revitalizing the small family room/dining nook pictured *above.* Here, periwinkle-blue paint has a captivating effect on the former all-neutral scheme. Chosen for its country French personality, the blue was picked up from the colorful rag rug and used to its fullest extent on the walls, woodwork, and two old wooden dining chairs.

The same shade of blue also ties together the mini-print fabric covering the sofa, the quilt-turned-tablecloth, and the striped material used for balloon shades and seat cushions. These coordinated fabrics introduce a counterpoint of pattern and other colors that keeps the basically blue scheme from becoming overwhelming.

DECORATING IN STAGES

Moving to a new house almost always entails taking on a redecorating project. Maybe the former owners' tastes in carpet and wall coverings are at odds with your own. Or perhaps you simply want to make a change. Few people who have just made a move can afford the expense of a major decorating project, but fortunately, it isn't necessary—or even advisable—to redo a room in one fell swoop. In fact, no matter what your finances, you may be better off to decorate a room in several stages. This case study demonstrates how one family, with the help of a designer, did just that.

When the owners of the suburban ranch house featured here moved in, they were greeted with a sea of white—carpet, walls, and window treatments, as shown in the inset *opposite.* Rather than try to decorate around something they didn't like, they sold the white carpet and replaced it with the gray industrial-style carpet pictured *at right.*

To balance this expense, the couple decided not to buy new furniture and accessories, but chose to re-cover existing pieces instead. Now gray fabric gives new life to the sofas. Accenting the sophisticated new scheme is a colorful decorator fabric—used boldly in the living room to cover two chairs and several toss pillows, and more subtly in the dining area, pictured *above,* for the table skirt. The new wall color echoes the rose hue in the floral fabric.

The overall effect looks appealing and pulled-together, but, as you'll see on the next two pages, there was more to come. *(continued)*

DECORATING IN STAGES
(continued)

The homeowners waited over a year before starting the second phase of their decorating project. The completed room, pictured *at right* and *above*, shows the impact artwork and accessories can have. An asymmetrical arrangement of framed posters and prints above the sofa accentuates the sloping lines of the lofty ceiling and adds color dynamics to the room. A handsomely framed and matted print above the dining area buffet brings interest to that section of the room.

Several new lamps—a swing-arm wall-mounted fixture; a simple, juglike table lamp with a white opaque shade; and a tall black torchère—not only infuse the setting with ambient light but also add variety.

Replacing the makeshift coffee table shown on the previous page is a contemporary black-and-white modular one that can be arranged to form a single round surface or, as shown here, separated into four wedge-shape segments.

Finishing touches in the dining area include a black polished-cotton top cloth for the table, a buffet which consists of two small units with smoked glass doors used together, and another swing-arm lamp like the one in the living room. The dining table, by the way, was fashioned from a half-sheet of ¾-inch plywood cut into a circle and fitted with screw-on dowel legs.

CONQUERING SPACE

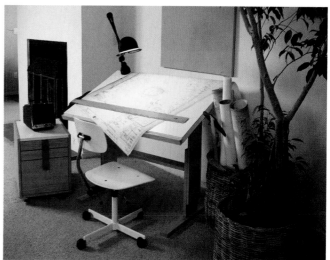

Every room, no matter what its size or shape, can be made to function in a variety of ways. So even if the floor plan of your house, condominium, or apartment is identical to that of your neighbors', you needn't be stymied by sameness. The most important thing is to choose and arrange furnishings so that they enrich your way of life—not just the way your surroundings look.

The living/dining room pictured *at left* is the twin of the room shown on the following pages. But as you'll discover, the two rooms not only look different, they also function in decidedly different ways.

Here the emphasis is on comfort and convenience. Casual furnishings, unconventionally arranged, provide an easygoing ambience for the young family that lives here. In order to make the space best suit their needs, the owners ignored the builder's floor plan and placed the dining area where the living area is "supposed" to be. Their reason for doing so was to create a cozy fireside eating spot where family members could also gather in the evenings to do hobbies, homework, and other projects. A large harvest-style dining table, with its easy-care surface, is an excellent choice for accommodating all of these functions. A drafting table shown *above*—arranged in its own corner with task lighting and efficient, compact storage—supplements the room's work space and creates an ideal mini-office. *(continued)*

123

CONQUERING SPACE
(continued)

It's hard to believe that the room pictured *at right* and *above* is identical in size and shape to the room featured on the preceding two pages. In the setting shown here, contemporary furnishings harmonize with mellow antiques and accessories for an eclectic, country-modern look. There's an air of elegance about the room, but the overall mood is soothing and relaxed.

Because the family that lives here likes to entertain frequently, the design emphasis is on plenty of comfortable seating pieces and easy access to the kitchen. As you can see, the arrangement is the reverse of the room pictured on pages 122 and 123: The conversation area focuses on the fireplace, and the dining area is placed in close proximity to the kitchen and outdoor terrace.

A modular L-shape sofa and a matching chaise longue offer the utmost in creature comfort and are easy to rearrange when need be. Extra seating is provided by a small sofa

placed next to the fireplace, pictured *above*. (In the room on the preceding two pages, a drafting table occupied this sliver of space.)

The dining end of this long, narrow room features a glass-topped pedestal table and four contemporary wicker chairs. When large parties are in progress, the table is moved toward the kitchen wall and put to use as a serve-yourself bar surface. Dining chairs are moved against the wall or into the fireside seating area, and the antique console to the right of the chaise longue becomes a buffet.

During warm-weather months, the French doors are usually open to encourage a flow of guests between the gracious indoor entertainment area and a well-tended garden. But whatever the weather, this room serves its purpose beautifully and well.

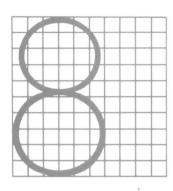

FINE-TUNING YOUR DECOR

At last, the basics are in place. Your furniture feels just right, the background is soothing and appealing, and your rooms are ready for a little decorative fine-tuning. These finishing touches—a sprinkling of well-loved treasures accentuated by just the right lighting—make the difference between a truly smashing room and one that's merely OK. Fortunately, there's nothing difficult about arranging accessories or coming up with a successful lighting plan. Just adapt the techniques outlined in this chapter.

ARRANGING ACCESSORIES

Any space—even a forgotten niche or wall—can become a distinctive decorative asset when you accessorize it boldly. A strip of track lighting and a few framed prints will transform dull hallways into galleries. One or more bold wall colors, a new poster, or an uplight tucked behind a floor plant will help turn a nondescript entry into one that's exciting. Even an ordinary tabletop becomes a conversation piece when you add special items that reflect your personality or hobbies.

Accessories can offer function as well as eye appeal, as shown in the grouping pictured *at right*. During parties, the sculptural sofa table becomes a bar or buffet, and the attractive stools offer extra seating.

To add impact and importance to this grouping of functional accents, a large Japanese triptych hangs above the table. The artwork echoes the horizontal lines of the table and injects color and pattern.

Choose complementary accessories

Balance needn't always mean symmetry. Some of the most delightful—and dynamic—groupings are asymmetrical. In the room shown here, something was needed to counterbalance the wider, heavier look of the triptych. The burled-wood pedestal provides the needed visual weight.

Even disparate items will "connect" beautifully if they have something in common. In this vignette, each item offers clean-lined simplicity. Equally important, common use of natural materials, such as clay, cotton, wood, and budding pussy willow sprigs, helps tie the mélange together.

(continued)

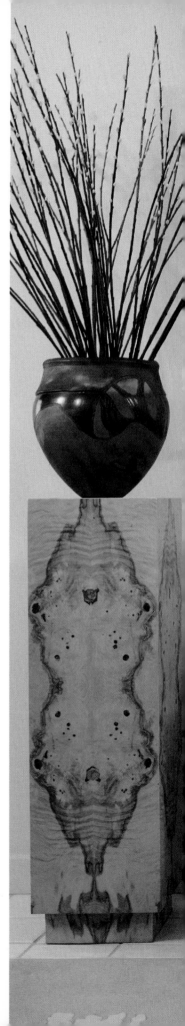

ARRANGING ACCESSORIES
(continued)

When it comes to arranging accessories, "editing" is the key to achieving a pleasing effect. Instead of using everything you have, selectively group only compatible items. Then refresh your eye by periodically putting away some things and bringing others out of storage.

These tips will help you plan arrangements.

• *Unite accents with color.* One way to turn a potential hodge-podge into a cohesive assemblage is with color. A clutter of seemingly unrelated elements will become a compatible "family" if you group only those of the same hue.

If your favorite color is green, for example, try assembling a mix of green accents on a shelf. You might start with a green bowl or bud vase, then add other green items (sculpture, a jar, pottery, whatever) as you find them.

One variation on this approach is to group items that share both color and materials. The tabletop grouping pictured *above* is a case in point. Jars and vases share a blue-and-white color scheme, and each also is of Oriental porcelain.

• *Group by mood or style to avoid clutter.* If you love to collect things but find your home looking cluttered, you may be spreading your accessories too thin. Instead of scattering similar items piecemeal around a room, gather them together on a table or shelf, or in a display cabinet. Not only will your home look less busy, but your treasures also will gain greater impact.

Compatibility may take many forms. If objects don't share

color, pattern, or shape, look for a similar style or feeling. You may prefer accents of one style—Oriental, contemporary, or eighteenth-century designs, for example. Another approach is to select accents that simply share a mood or feeling. Handmade items—examples of fine stitchery, pottery, or woodworking, for instance—may appeal to you, or perhaps you find yourself drawn to organic materials—dried flowers and weeds, or naturally sculpted driftwood.

The owners of the family room shown *at right* have added down-home warmth with country accessories. Blue-and-white spatterware and porcelain repeat the upholstery colors, and, for a touch of whimsy, wooden birds from cock to canary take roost around the room.

DISPLAYING ARTWORK

Well-loved artwork—be it your children's watercolors from school or a special limited-edition print—often provides the perfect finishing touch to any room. Although few rigid rules apply when hanging and arranging works of art, these guidelines will ensure success.

Before you hang anything *on* your walls, consider the walls themselves. If you have patterned wallpaper, for example, create important breathing space between the artwork and the wall with wide mats and frames. If paint is your choice, don't be afraid to try a rich hue. In many cases, a dark or intense wall color will highlight artwork beautifully.

Arrangement pointers
It's usually best to hang a very large or special work alone to give it the attention it deserves. But if you have several smaller or related items, a grouping of artworks may be best. Such clusters can be keyed by color, subject matter, or framing technique. For best results, vary the sizes and shapes of the elements. In the handsome living room shown *at right,* a collection of varisized drawings is linked both by its architectural subject matter and by matching frames and mats.

To keep any arrangement from looking haphazard, plan to have one or two straight lines running through the grouping, and create a clean, geometric shape with the outer edges of the grouping. Also, to make sure your arrangement "hangs together," limit the space between items to a few inches.

The way you hang your artwork also can help you make the most of your space. In the room shown here, the to-the-ceiling placement creates a dramatic feeling of height and draws the eye to the intricate ceiling molding. In a narrow room, a horizontal grouping on either of the end walls will help add an illusion of width. Or, if your ceiling is too high, bring it down by hanging your artwork at a cozy, low level.

(continued)

DISPLAYING ARTWORK
(continued)

One of the most effective ways to display art objects is also one of the easiest. Choose only two or three special items per room and give each piece a starring role on its own, carefully allotted "stage." After all, any treasured work—be it an oil painting or perhaps a blowup of one of your favorite vacation snapshots—can deserve special prominence.

In the room shown *above* one focal-point painting commands attention on the far wall. The piece is hung at a low level so it can be especially appreciated from a seated position. In the left-hand corner of the room, a piece of sculp-ture shows off its form against an absolutely plain background. Breathing room keeps the pieces from competing for recognition.

In this arrangement the vertical visual "weight" of the sculpture atop its tall pedestal counterbalances the strong horizontals of the painting and sofas below it.

Amassing the unexpected
Instead of savoring one item at a time by letting it perform solo, you might prefer to personalize your place with a large grouping of uncommon works of art. In the living room pictured *opposite,* a selection of quilts arranged on a custom-built wooden wall rack lends one-of-a-kind style to a countrified scheme. Quilts easily can be rearranged or exchanged for others in the owner's collection whenever a change of pace is desired. Shades of gray on walls, floor, and furnishings combine to create a neutral backdrop for a variety of color schemes. In this array, a disparate pattern mix is linked by the color red.

Keeping balance in mind
Whenever you're arranging artwork and accessories, keep balance in mind. A large painting or grouping of colorful accents like these quilts demands counterbalancing elsewhere in the room. A few coordinated accessories will help distribute color throughout a space.

In this room, a quilt draped over a pine bench connects the art on the wall with the furnishings and serves as a subtle reminder of the functional nature of these works of art.

CHOOSING LIGHTING

If you still think of lighting as simply a couple of matching table lamps flanking your sofa and a reading lamp next to your favorite lounge chair, you're missing a lot of fun and drama. Thanks to a growing range of excellent portable and built-in lighting products available to the general public, sophisticated lighting *is* within your grasp. Here and on the following two pages, we'll describe some products and techniques that will help you see your rooms in the right light.

Many terrific rooms go dull at night. But that doesn't have to be the case. With a little planning, you can imbue your home with sparkling nighttime drama. Since all good lighting plans start with *function,* be sure you know what you want to accomplish before you shop for lighting products.

• Is your room a place for quiet conversation, music-listening, or TV-watching? Perhaps all you need here are warm pools of accent lighting to invite you into and guide you through the space.

• Will you want to read, handle paperwork and correspondence, work on hobbies, or play games in the room? If so, you'll want to provide adequate task lights—reading lamps where necessary and perhaps adjustable downlights over hobby or writing tables.

• Is an area primarily a daytime or nighttime space? If it's a daytime room, consider its exposure to the sun. A south-facing room may need little auxiliary lighting, while a north-facing one will benefit from warm lamplight.

If you work during the day and use your rooms mostly at night, aim for a mix of lighting types. In the home pictured *at left,* the dining room doubles for nocturnal desk work. A portable Tizio lamp (see page 136) provides flexible task light; spotlights on an over-head track add general illumination.

Equally important to the table light is the background glow from incandescent tubes recessed beneath the book-shelves. These accent lights create a balance of light throughout the space, add an illusion of greater depth, and, of course, make it easy to find reading material at night.

(continued)

CHOOSING
LIGHTING
(continued)

Remember that lighting can change the apparent dimensions of a room. "Enlarge" a space by washing walls with floodlights on a track. Add a feeling of height by bouncing light off the ceiling from a torchère or uplights concealed in a cornice. Or open up a corner instantly with a plug-in uplight.

You can "cozy up" with lighting, too. Add low-level accent lights to a tall space or create intimacy in a large room by placing lamps well within the room's actual perimeter.

Putting it all together

The room shown here offers lots of adaptable ideas. Thanks to subtle, concisely focused lighting, art objects seem to glow from within. Besides saving energy, the low-voltage ceiling fixtures project intense, controlled beams of light. Depending on the bulbs used, the beams range from narrow pin spots to wider wall-washers. Broad beams center on the large framed drawing, while tiny pinspots set small objects aglow.

The array of ceiling lights in the photo *opposite* is a custom installation, but you can achieve a similar effect with standard fixtures on a regular track.

More flexible light is supplied by the Tizio lamp—a sculptural update of the classic architect's lamp. Fitted with a low-energy, high-wattage and high-intensity halogen bulb, the lamp has a movable head, flexible arm, and pivoting base that lets it serve for reading, wall washing, or highlighting art objects. Finally, fluorescent tubes mounted in the sofa base make it seem to float, and tiny plug-in lamps made for planters open up a dark corner.

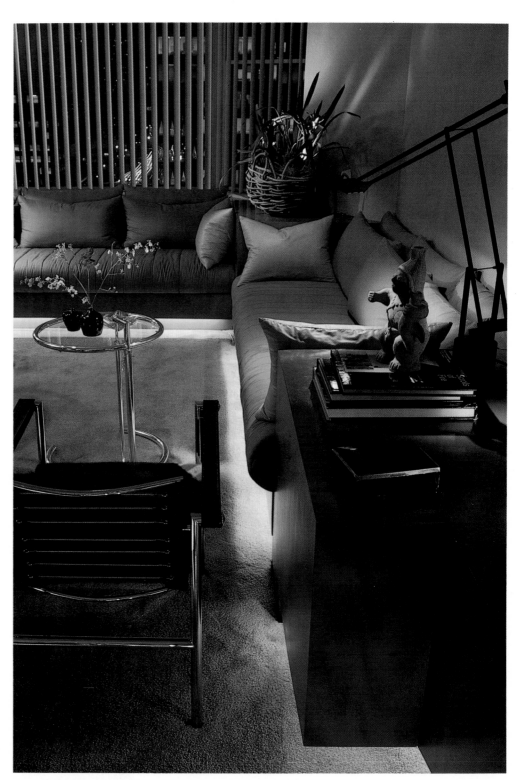

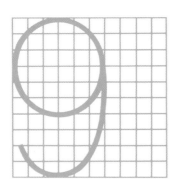

SEWING FOR YOUR HOME

A modest investment in a sewing machine yields multiple benefits. Not only can you save hundreds of dollars when you sew your own accessories, you also can have curtains, shades, cushions, and table coverings in fabrics perfectly coordinated to your color scheme. To ensure success, choose a suitable weight of fabric: too flimsy and it won't last; too stiff and it will be hard to sew and may not drape properly. Preshrink all washable materials and trims. The projects featured in this chapter are all simple to make and require only basic sewing skills. If you're a novice, you can get detailed sewing information where you buy your fabrics.

To give handmade window treatments a professionally fitted look, install rods first, then measure down to where you want the curtains to end. If you're using curtain rings, measure from the bottom of the rings. Then, measure the width of the rod from bracket to bracket. These two measurements are the keys to good-fitting window coverings.

For a shirred curtain, shown *opposite, left,* allow 9½ inches of fabric at the top for the casing and heading, 6 inches at the bottom for a doubled hem. Plan panel widths that will total about 2½ times the rod length plus 4 inches for each doubled side hem.

If necessary, stitch panels together to achieve the width you need. Press under and stitch a doubled 2-inch hem at each side and a doubled 3-inch hem at the bottom.

Turn the fabric under 5 inches at the upper edge. Press under ½ inch on the raw edge and stitch through all thicknesses close to the fold. Stitch again 2 inches above the first row to create a rod casing.

Traditional pleated draperies, *opposite, center,* are made with pleater tape, hooks, lining, and drapery weights. To figure how much fabric you need, pleat a strip of the tape with hooks until you've reached the desired drapery width. Remove pins, unpleat, and measure the tape's length. Add to this the space of rod returns *plus* 4 inches for overlap at the center of two panels and, for doubled side hems, 4 inches for each outside side panel.

To the finished length, add 7 inches. Cut lining fabric 6 inches shorter and 3 inches narrower than the face fabric. Add 1 inch for each piecing seam.

Cut fabric lengths and stitch them to the required width. Stitch a doubled 3-inch hem at the drapery bottom, a doubled 1-inch hem at the lining bottom.

Place right sides of lining and drapery fabric together; pin and stitch ½-inch side seams. Turn and press, positioning the lining 1½ inches in from folded edges.

Lay pleater tape on top edge of the drapery fabric, overlapping ½ inch and extending ½ inch at each side. Stitch. Fold tape back so it lies against the lining, allowing ½ inch between the tape and the top of the drapery. Fold under overhanging tape and stitch it to the lining's edge. Stitch along the bottom edge of pleater tape. Insert hooks.

The tieback, *opposite, right,* is made much like the shirred curtain described above. For curtains that hang on one section of a double rod, allow 2½ inches at the top for a rod casing, 6 inches at the bottom for a doubled 3-inch hem. If you plan to add an eyelet border (as we did), take its width into account in figuring panel sizes.

Make the total width about 2½ times the rod length plus 4 inches per panel for hemming. Press under and stitch a doubled 2-inch hem at each side and a doubled 3-inch hem at the bottom. Turn the top edge under ½ inch and then again 2 inches; stitch close to the fold to form the rod casing.

Plan the finished valance to be about ⅛ the length of the finished curtain. Cut and stitch following directions for the shirred curtain discussed at left. If you add eyelet trim, allow for the length it adds.

Cut a 7x21-inch piece for each tieback. Fold in half lengthwise; stitch, leaving an opening for turning. Turn to right side; press. Secure using cup hooks and plastic rings.

SHADES

All the shades shown here pull up with cords. Each is mounted to a board at the top, with a metal rod at the bottom for weight.

The pleated balloon shade, *near right,* adds softness in pleats. To determine the number of pleats, divide the window width by 12. Cut fabric to finished width measurements plus 12 inches for each double pleat, 6 inches for each single side pleat and 2 inches for side hems. Cut to the desired finished length, plus 2 inches each for a bottom hem and top mounting allowance.

Purchase ring tape to equal the finished length of the shade times the total number of pleats. Each shade also requires lift cord, ⅜-inch metal rod the width of the window, and a rod casing of self fabric or 1-inch twill tape.

Turn under and stitch doubled ½-inch hems at the sides; make a doubled 1-inch hem at the bottom. Sew ring tape to the wrong side of fabric ½ inch in from the sides and over the center of each double pleat. Pin and press pleats. Finish the pleated top edge with large zigzag stitches. Sew a rod casing at the bottom of the shade; insert rod.

Staple the shade to the wide side of a 1x2 board cut to fit the window. Install screw eyes on the board's underside above each row of ring tape. For each row of rings, cut a lift cord long enough to tie to the bottom ring, pass through all rings on the tape, through the screw eyes and halfway down one side of the shade. Screw the board to the window frame. Attach an awning cleat to the frame to secure the cords.

The cloud shade, *center,* is soft and poufy even when it's down. Cut fabric twice the width and 1½ times the length of the window. Stitch purchased shirring tape to the shade's top hemmed edge. Instead of ring tape, sew ½-inch plastic rings on inside of the shade; space them equally—6 to 10 inches lengthwise, 18 inches widthwise. Pull up on shirring tape stitching to gather to the desired width. Staple the shade to a 1x2, and rig cords as with the balloon shade. Insert a rod in the bottom hem.

The lined Roman shade, *far right,* is sewn to fit the width of the window exactly. Allow for hems when cutting fabric; a double 4-inch hem at the bottom will conceal a rod casing in back. Use ring tape and cords as in the balloon shade.

All the pillows shown here are variations on a theme. They are all made in the easiest way—two pieces of fabric stitched together. We used pillow forms for the stuffing; if you choose loose fill, sew it in a muslin liner to make washing easier.

The basic knife-edge pillows on and next to the love seat are made from identically sized pieces of fabric. Stitch (we used ½ inch seams for everything) with right sides together, leaving an opening on one side for stuffing. Trim corners, turn to the right side, and press. Insert a pillow form and slip-stitch the opening.

The solid pink flange pillowcase on the chaise covers a 12x18-inch bed pillow. Because it's made with a zipper in the back, the front and back are cut differently. Cut the front with 2½ inches extra all around (17x23 inches). Cut two back pieces 13x17 inches. Install a zipper and seam together so the front and back pieces will be the same size. Open the zipper and sew front to back, right sides together. To make the flange, turn to the right side, press, and machine-stitch 2 inches from the outer edge.

The Turkish corner pillows, also on the chaise, are another variation of the knife-edge style. Cut and stitch as you

would a knife-edge pillow, but before turning to the right side, baste a diagonal line 3 inches from each corner. Pull up stitches to gather fabric along these lines. Machine-zigzag along the basting line to hold gathering in place. Trim the corners, turn to the right side, stuff, and stitch the opening.

For the ruffled-edge pillow, also on the chaise, cut and stitch a basic knife-edge pillow, and cut ruffle strips 1½ inches wider than the desired ruffle and 2½ times the perimeter measurement of the pillow. Turn under both edges of this strip ¼ inch twice and stitch. Run rows of long machine stitching ½ and ¾ inch from one edge. Pull up stitching to equal the pillow's perimeter. Pin the ruffle to the outside edge of the pillow front and stitch through all thicknesses except over the opening, where you hand-stitch the ruffle in place. Insert a pillow form and stitch closed.

The chair cushion, left foreground, features corded edges and ties that secure it to the chair. To make a pattern, trace around the chair seat and add a ½-inch seam allowance. Cut two fabric pieces with the pattern and cut bias strips to cover the cording. Stitch these over the cording and then to one piece of the pillow face. From 5-inch-wide bias pieces, make the ties by folding the fabric in half, right sides together, and stitching; turn. Pin the ties in place and then stitch the corded pillow face to the other pillow face with right sides together, leaving an opening between the ties for turning. Trim seams and clip curves; turn to the right side, insert a pillow form, and stitch closed.

TABLE COVERINGS

To make mix-and-match table coverings like the collection pictured here, choose washable fabrics for dining tables; decorative overskirts for other tables need not be washable. Sheets make ideal fabrics because of their width. Where seaming is necessary, allow extra fabric for matching prints. Avoid placing a seam directly across the center.

Besides the plain hems shown here, you can experiment with ruffles, welts, scalloped and pleated edges, and purchased trims. Complement your tablecloths with fabric napkins and place mats.

A round tablecloth can be cut as shown in the diagram. Its total diameter should equal the width of the table plus twice the distance to the floor, plus 1 inch for the hem and 1 inch for any seam needed. Fold and pin the fabric in quarters. Use tape or string like a compass and mark the cutting line. Cut through all thicknesses at once. Finish with a ½-inch hem. Machine-stitch all around the edge with two rows of large stitches ½ inch and then ¼ inch from the edge. Pull slightly on the stitches and steam lightly to draw up the curved hem, then machine-stitch through both layers.

A square cloth often has a drop of 10 to 12 inches at the sides, but it can go to any length. For floor length, trim corners to a curve. Determine how big a cloth you want and add ½ inch on all sides. Finish with a narrow hem.

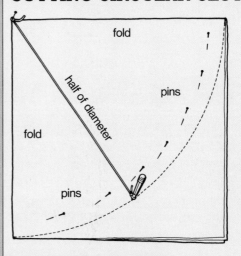

CUTTING CIRCULAR CLOTH

fold

fold

half of diameter

pins

pins

four edges

Brighten a kid's room with the practical, easy-to-make ideas shown here.

Pattern a new director's chair cover on the old chair cover. If you use a medium-weight fabric, reinforce it by stitching it to canvas backing.

For tailored bedcovers, cut prequilted fabric like fitted sheets. Measure mattress top and sides with sheets and covers on. Add 4 inches of fabric on all sides. Stitch mitered corners; sew elastic to the underside of each. Cover edges with double-fold bias tape.

Pillows are versions of the flange pillows shown on page 142. Allow extra fabric to apply Velcro instead of a zipper at the closing.

For each storage pocket, cut two pieces of heavyweight fabric to the size of the pocket plus ½ inch for seams on three sides and 6 inches on the back for tucking in under the mattress. Stitch, right sides together, leaving an opening for turning. For the pocket section, cut fabric twice the width of the backing plus 4 inches. Fold in half with right side together and stitch around three sides. Fold pleats as desired to create the pocket. Pin in place and topstitch fabric around three sides and vertically to divide pocket sections. Apply Velcro to the mattress bottom and to the pocket strip. The large pocket is made with straps at the top. Use Velcro strips on strap ends and the pocket back.

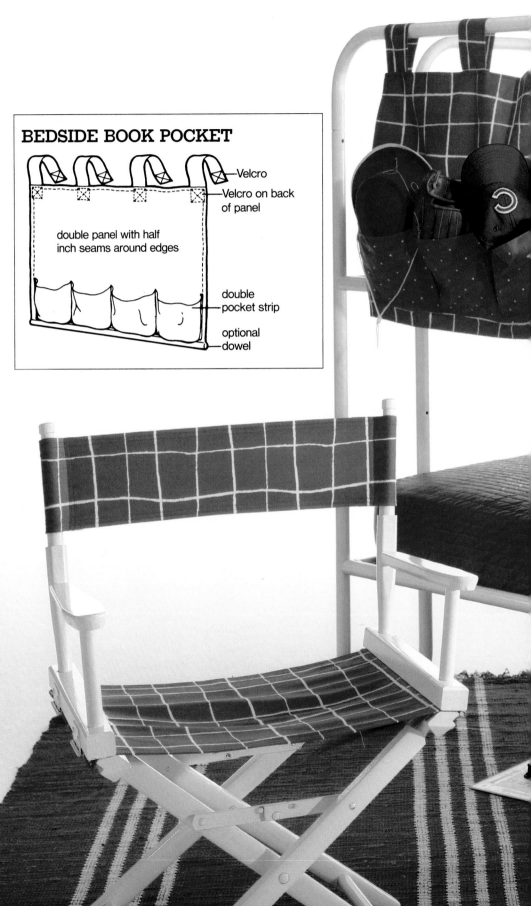

BEDSIDE BOOK POCKET

Velcro

Velcro on back of panel

double panel with half inch seams around edges

double pocket strip

optional dowel

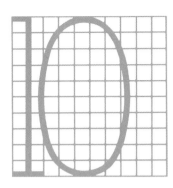

WHEN TO STOP

When it comes to good design, what you leave out has as much to do with success as what you put in. This chapter deals with one of the most valuable decorating tools: restraint. Here you'll find sound advice that can help you know when to stop decorating a room.

LEAVE SOME BREATHING ROOM

One key element to include in your decorating plans is both invisible and free: breathing room. Much more than mere "dead" or "undecorated" space, true breathing space is a positive, almost tangible feature.

Leave some floor and wall surfaces open, and you'll be better able to appreciate the shapes, colors, and textures of each of your carefully chosen furniture pieces and accessories.

Suppose, for example, you've purchased a painting or lithograph by a favorite artist. Sandwich it into a grouping between many other works, and your treasure may well be buried. Mount it alone on a blank wall with lots of space around it, and it will get the attention it deserves.

Let open spaces showcase forms and textures

Against a whitewashed backdrop, the curvilinear forms and tactile qualities of the furnishings and accents in the room pictured *at right* come beautifully to the fore.

With nothing to stand in its way, a twig rocking chair—folk art you can really use—shows off its gracefully bowed back. Twilled cotton upholstery and a striking sisal rug bring visual and tactile interest to a room that might otherwise seem cold and stark. In a stagelike setting such as this, a cactus gains the impact of sculpture. Special accents—in this case, a prized collection of American Indian blankets (like the ones in the print hung above one sofa)—are fully seen and, thus, fully appreciated.

USE WALL COVERINGS JUDICIOUSLY

Few things can warm up—or overpower—a room as quickly as wall coverings. The key to using wall coverings successfully is to first decide whether you want to emphasize walls or whether they would work better as subtle backgrounds. Success also depends on how well the pattern of the wall covering works with your furnishings and accessories. Whatever your wall-covering choice, remember that it should enhance, but never overwhelm, a room.

The owners of the new contemporary home whose master bedroom is shown *above* knew just what they wanted when they shopped for wall coverings: a warm, down-home look updated with fresh pastels. The fondant-color stripes they chose lend a decidedly old-fashioned, wainscotinglike appearance to the sloping walls.

This room also shows how wall coverings, when used judiciously, can accent architectural assets. By playing up the cozy slope of the ceiling, this wall covering imbues a modern, vaulted space with the character of a barn loft or country cottage.

Your home may have unusual or inconvenient architectural features that you want to minimize rather than emphasize. The wallpaper you choose can help do that. For example, to create a smooth, expansive look in a cut-up space, wallpaper doors as well as walls. Or use an all-over mini-print—not a stripe or grid—to play down awkward nooks, niches, and ceiling angles.

Creating a mood

In the room pictured *at right,* a trompe l'oeil trellis design, delicately embellished with a leafy, flowering vine, works well with formal French furnishings without upstaging them. In fact, the creamy-white background provides a sun-kissed glow and unexpectedly lighthearted, gazebolike setting for ornate items such as the heavily carved and painted table, and the leather-upholstered Louis XVI chair.

By not adding lots of wicker or floral accents, the designer stopped short of overdoing the garden theme. Instead, the wallpaper itself sets the mood, with only a few subtle accents to quietly reinforce the open-air feeling.

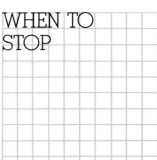

WHEN TO STOP

AVOID COLOR CACOPHONY

Nature has a deft hand when it comes to using colors. A garden's floral mix or autumn's riot of changing reds and golds never appear overdone. Somehow, it isn't so easy to mix colors in our homes. How can you avoid contrived schemes? Here are some helpful guidelines.

There are as many kinds of color schemes as there are hues themselves. From monochromatic serenity to basically white rooms punched up with bold primary-color artwork, the choice is yours.

The kitchen pictured *at left* gains its restful appeal from an unexpected mix of soft colors. Blue and gray cabinets, peach trim, and dark marble all share gray undertones.

Subtlety is the key to a successful grayed-down scheme like this. Lots of pastel accents could easily have turned a just-right color mix into a contrived one. Instead, the owners rely on texture for added interest: fibrous woven chairs, rough pottery, and wood accents.

A large dose of strong color may seem like too much of a good thing, but not when the colors are intermixed as handsomely as they are in the living room shown *above*. What keeps this powerful palette from clashing? All the colors are tints or shades of red, each subtly toned down with underlying brown shading. Each color, from brick to bisque, represents today's rich earth tones—colors derived from desert sunsets, clay pots, and rocky outcroppings.

In any strong scheme like this, rely on solid neutrals for visual balance. Here, the plain-white woodwork, lamps, table base, and ceiling keep the rich colors in check.

WHEN TO STOP

PRUNE YOUR PATTERNS

Rooms do not live by color alone. Most need at least a touch of pattern for real decorative punch. But how much? Again, you must start by deciding the kind of mood you want to create. A restful scheme usually demands subtle, unobtrusive designs—perhaps with more reliance on tactile variety than on pattern interplay. But if a stimulating mood is what you prefer, bolder colors and patterns may be just right. The two eye-catching examples here offer ideas to get you started.

In most cases, two or three patterns are about all a room can handle before things get too busy. Even mixing a couple of patterns takes a careful eye. Often, you'll find that choosing very different designs (say, a stripe and a floral print) that share matching colors is your best bet. It's usually wise to let one pattern dominate, then use one or two secondary patterns as accents.

One way to link a mix is with scale. The dining area pictured *above,* for example, gains its charm from a yellow-and-blue mini-print wallpaper. Note how the place mats have complementary, small-scale blue and white stripes.

In any patterned scheme, solids provide necessary relief for the eye. Here, the plain pine table, red canvas chair slings and vinyl floor serve that role beautifully.

If you're unsure about mixing patterns on your own, let premixed collections of wall coverings and fabrics remove the guesswork. For example, the country bedroom shown *at right* owes much of its cozy charm to four related prints from one such collection.

154

Better Homes and Gardens® Books

Would you like to learn more about decorating, remodeling, or maintaining your home? These Better Homes and Gardens® books can help.

Better Homes and Gardens®
NEW DECORATING BOOK

How to translate ideas into workable solutions for every room in your home. Choosing a style, furniture arrangements, windows, walls and ceilings, floors, lighting, and accessories. 433 color photos, 76 how-to illustrations, 432 pages.

Better Homes and Gardens®
COMPLETE GUIDE TO HOME REPAIR,
MAINTENANCE & IMPROVEMENT

Inside your home, outside your home, your home's systems, basics you should know. Anatomy and step-by-step drawings illustrate components, tools, techniques, and finishes. 515 how-to techniques; 75 charts; 2,734 illustrations; 552 pages.

Better Homes and Gardens®
COMPLETE GUIDE TO GARDENING

A comprehensive guide for beginners and experienced gardeners. Houseplants, lawns and landscaping, trees and shrubs, greenhouses, insects and diseases. 461 color photos, 434 how-to illustrations, 37 charts, 552 pages.

Better Homes and Gardens®
STEP-BY-STEP BUILDING SERIES

A series of do-it-yourself building books that provides step-by-step illustrations and how-to information for starting and finishing many common construction projects and repair jobs around your house. More than 90 projects and 1,200 illustrations in this series of six 96-page books:
STEP-BY-STEP BASIC PLUMBING
STEP-BY-STEP BASIC WIRING
STEP-BY-STEP BASIC CARPENTRY
STEP-BY-STEP HOUSEHOLD REPAIRS
STEP-BY-STEP MASONRY & CONCRETE
STEP-BY-STEP CABINETS & SHELVES

Other Sources of Information

Many professional and special-interest associations publish catalogs, style books, or product brochures that are available upon request.

American Society of Interior Designers (ASID)
730 Fifth Avenue
New York, NY 10019

American Furniture Manufacturers Association
P.O. Box HP-7
High Point, NC 27261

American Home Lighting Institute
435 North Michigan Avenue
Chicago, IL 60611

Carpet and Rug Institute
P.O. Box 2048
Dalton, GA 30720

General Electric Answer Center
(800) 626-2000

National Association of Furniture Manufacturers
8401 Connecticut Ave, Suite 911
Washington, DC 20015

ACKNOWLEDGMENTS

Architects and Designers

The following is a listing, by page, of the interior designers, architects, and project designers whose work appears in this book.

Cover:
Ann Clark
Pages 6–7
Robert A.M. Stern, Ronald Bricke & Associates
Pages 8–9
Gary Owens, AIA
Pages 10–11
Trisha Wilson, ASID
Pages 12–13
Robert E. Dittmer
Pages 14–15
Jane Siris and Peter Coombs
Pages 16–17
Jenice Gram
Pages 18–19
Thomas Boccia
Pages 20–21
Don York
Pages 22–23
Robert E. Dittmer
Pages 24–25
Jacque Campbell; Pamela Hughes & Co.
Pages 26–27
Jeffrey Charnok
Pages 28–29
Ristomatti Ratia

Pages 30–31
Alice Eckley
Pages 32–33
R. Thomas Gunkelman, ASID; Bette Zakarian
Pages 34–35
Alice Eckley; John and Anne Houser
Pages 36–37
Douglas Atwill
Pages 38–39
Sam Anthony Cardella
Pages 42–43
Raymond Waites
Pages 64–65
Lois Lugonja
Pages 64–65
Rosenthal-Rubbico Associates Inc.; John and Anne Houser
Pages 66–67
Bill Hopkins, Jr.; Robert Etz, ASID
Pages 68–69
Luis Ortega; Robert E. Dittmer
Pages 70–71
Louise Rosenfeld, Arrangements, Inc.; Darrel Schmitt, ASID
Pages 72–73
Carol Kaplan, Two by Two Interior Design; Pineapple House, John Lundgren Interiors
Pages 74–75
Cynthia, Inc.
Pages 76–77
Suzy Stout
Pages 78–79
Carolyn Guttilla/Plaza One; Marilyn Hannigan
Pages 80–81
Ruth Temple Touhill

Pages 82–83
Stephen A. Savage
Pages 84–85
Robert E. Dittmer
Pages 86–87
Suzy Stout
Pages 88–89
Phillip Young
Pages 90–91
R. Thomas Gunkelman, ASID
Pages 92–93
Margot Ladwig
Pages 106–109
Ann Clark
Pages 110–113
Robert E. Dittmer; Sara Seldin
Pages 114–115
Morley Smith
Pages 116–117
Joyce Griffith, Judith Morgan, Papier Interiors, Inc.; Sharon Sawyer
Pages 118–123
Robert E. Dittmer
Pages 124–125
Carolyn Guttilla
Pages 126–127
Robert W. Turner, Design Source
Pages 128–129
Carol Leverett and Beverly Field; Suzy Stout
Pages 130–131
Susanne Adams

Pages 132–133
Larry Deutsch, ASID
Pages 134–137
David Winfield Wilson; Scott Himmel, AIA
Pages 138–147
Stephen Mead Associates
Pages 148–149
Bill Yoe & Associates
Pages 150–151
Ann Levine and Bryan McCay; Scott Lamb
Pages 152–153
Charles Morris Mount; Jois Belfied
Page 154
Robert E. Dittmer

Photographers and Illustrators

We extend our thanks to the following photographers and illustrators, whose creative talents and technical skills contributed to this book.

Ross Chapple
George de Gennaro
Hedrich-Blessing
Thomas Hooper
Hopkins Associates
Fred Lyon
Maris/Semel
E. Alan McGee
Carson Ode
Bradley Olman
Jim Peck
John Rogers
John Vaughan
Jessie Walker
Bruce Wolf

DECORATING YOUR HOME

INDEX

Page numbers in *italics* refer to illustrations or illustrated text.

A–B

Accessories, 18, *19, 23, 60–61*
  arranging, *126–129*
  in color scheme, *76–78*
  combining, *24*
  for personal style, *92–93*
  romantic decorating, *42–45*
  with spaces around, *148–149*
Adaptation of old pieces, 30
American Society of Interior Designers (ASID), 104
Antiques, sources of, 98, *99*
Architectural details
  emphasizing, *88–89, 150*
  minimizing, 150
Architectural salvage firms, 103
Armoire, *22–23*
Arrangement
  of accessories, *126–129*
  of artwork, *130–131*
  of room *58–59, 84–85*
Artwork
  ancestral portrait, *27*
  Chinese screen, *21*
  displaying, *130–133*
  Japanese triptych, *126–127*
  lighting, *137*
  posters, *85, 106, 121*
  prints, *32, 90–91, 121, 149*
  watercolors, *41*
Auctions, 98
Balloon shade, *140*
Barcelona chairs, *32–33, 38–39*
Barcelona table, *32–33*
Baskets, wall-hung, *19*
Bay windows, *38–39*
  treatments for, *74*
Beamed ceilings, *36–37, 66–67*
Bedcovers for children, *146–147*

Bedrooms
  ceiling, trellis-patterned, *66*
  children's, accessories for, *146–147*
  color use in, *78–79*
  fabric use in, *86–87*
  handcrafted furniture, *36*
  judicious use of wall coverings in, *150–151*
  lighting, *17*
  paint use in, *116–117*
  patterned walls, *64, 65, 154–155*
  romantic look, *42–43*
  starting-out scheme, *108*
  stripped-down look, *90–91*
  timelessness in, *30–31*
Beds
  with box spring on floor, *90–91*
  four-poster, *36, 79*
    pencil-post, *30–31*
  iron-and-brass, *86–87, 116–117*
  platform, *42–43, 113*
Bedside storage pockets, *146–147*
Bentwood chairs, *24–25*
Blinds, mini-slat, 72, *73, 90*
  with old pieces, *30*
Book pockets, bedside, *146–147*
Bookshelves, lights recessed beneath, *134–135*
Breakfast corner, *6–7*

C–D

Cabinets, kitchen, gray undertones for, *152–153*
Candlesticks, *44–45*
Carpet
  for dens, *70–71*
  industrial-style, *118–119*
Catalog shopping, 97
Ceiling lights, *137*
Ceilings, *66–67*
  beamed, *36–37, 66–67*
  wall covering on, *66, 150*
Chairs
  armless, *110–111*
  Barcelona, *32–33, 38–39*
  bentwood, *24–25*
  bergère, *83–83*
  boudoir, *116*
  cushion for, *142,* 143

Chairs (contd.)
  director's, *106–107, 146*
  Haitian cotton, *88–89*
  ladder-back, *9, 40–41*
  Louis XVI, *150*
  Mies van der Rohe-style, *14*
  nail-studded, leather, *38*
  with ottoman, wood-and-rush, *14*
  re-covered, *119, 121*
  Scandinavian wedding chairs, *28, 29*
  sling, canvas, *154*
  stackable, *112*
  tubular, *10–11*
  twig rocking chair, *149*
  upholstery fabric on, *22–23, 77*
  wicker, *71, 125*
  Windsor, *31*
  wing, *9, 22–23, 55*
  woven, in kitchen, *152–153*
Chaise longue, *125*
Changes, decorating, 44–61
  analysis before, 46
  arrangement of pieces, *58–59*
  backgrounds, 52–53
  completion of, with accessories, *60–61*
  key elements, introducing, 54
  lighting, *56–57*
  selectivity in, 51
  starting point, 48
Children's accessories, sewing, *146–147*
Cloud shade, *140–141*
Coffee tables. See Tables: coffee
Colonial-style rooms
  dining rooms, *24, 26–27*
  living room *76–77*
Color, use of, *78–79*
  for background treatments, 52–53
  in design collections, 100
  neutral plus one color, *80–81*
  pastels, *42–43*
  redecorating choices, 54
  restraint in, *152–153*

Color (contd.)
  single color family, *82–83, 153*
  for uniting accents, *128*
  for walls, *62–63*
Corner cupboards, *26, 35*
Corner pillows, 142–143, *143*
Cupboards
  barrow-back, *30–31*
  corner, *26, 35*
  in kitchen, *34*
Curtains, *138–139*
Cushion, chair, *142,* 143
Decorating
  accessorizing, See Accessories
  architectural details, emphasizing, *88–89, 150*
  arrangement of accessories, *126–129*
  arrangement of room, *58–59, 84–85*
  case studies, 106–125
    budgeting, *110–113*
    improving on present scheme, *114–117*
    space, using, to suit needs, *122–125*
    staged decorating, *118–121*
    starting from scratch, *106–109*
  with color. See Color, use of
  design professionals, use of 20, 104
  display of artwork, *130–133*
  extent of, determining, 8
  fabric, use of, *76–77*
    single pattern, *86–87*
  lighting considerations, *16–17, 56–57, 134–137*
  personal style, achieving, *92–93*
  reasons for, analyzing, 6, 46
  restraint in, 148–155
    breathing space, *148–149*
    color, use of, *152–153*
    pattern, use of, *154–155*
    wall coverings, *150–151*
  space considerations, *14–15*
  stripped-down look, *90–91*
  See also Changes, decorating; Sewing projects; Sources of supply; Style

Dens, carpet for, *70–71*
Department stores, 94
Design collections, 100, *101*
Design professionals, use of, 20, 104
Dhurrie rugs, *69, 84–85, 106–107, 115*
Dining areas, *112*
    paint use in, *117*
    pattern use in, *154*
    staged decorating, *118, 120*
Dining/living areas, *14–15*
    arrangement of, *84–85*
    individualized use of space, *122–125*
Dining rooms
    with accessories, *18–19*
    combination of elements in, *24–25*
    handcrafted items in, *35*
    with mini-slat blinds, *72–73*
    simplicity in, *26–27*
    starting-out scheme, *106–107*
    timeless look, *33*
    use for desk work, *134–135*
Director's chairs, *106–107, 146*
Display houses, 103
Doors, French, *7, 13, 45, 72, 125*
Drafting tables, *112–113, 123*
Draperies, 138, *139*
    French doors with, *45*
    tie-back, *72*
Drum as coffee table, *78*
Dust ruffle, floral, *86–87*

E–L

Eclectic living rooms, *38–41*
Fabrics, use of, *76–77*
    single-pattern, *86–87*
Family rooms
    country accessories in, *128–129*
    paint use in, *117*
Fireplaces, *39–41*
Flange pillowcase, 142, *143*
Floorcloth, *45*
Floors, *68–71*
    tile, *18–19, 66–67, 69*

Four-poster beds, *36–79*
    pencil-post, *30–31*
French doors, *7, 13, 45, 72, 125*
French furnishings, *150–151*
Handcrafts, schemes built around, *34–37*
Highboy, colonial-style, *87*
Home stores, 94
Hooked rug, *24*
Hutches, *19, 84*
Import shops, 103
Interior designers, use of, 20, 104
Kitchens
    breakfast corner, *6–7*
    color use in, *152–153*
    handcrafted items in, *34*
Knife-edge pillows, *142–143*
Ladder-back chairs, *9, 40–41*
Lamps, *120–121*
    with fabric shades, *86–87*
    hanging, *84*
    swing-arm reading lamps, *90*
    Tizio, *134, 136*
Lattice panels, *57*
Lighting, *16*, 56, *134–137*
    track lighting, *17, 21, 32–33, 56–57*
Living areas
    with dining areas, arrangement of, *84–85*
    individualized use of space, *122–125*
    neutral-plus-one-color scheme in, *80–81*
Living rooms
    apartment, *110–111, 114–115*
    architecture, emphasizing, *88–89*
    with beamed ceiling, *36–37, 66–67*
    color, use of, *78*
        single color family, *82–83, 153*
        for walls, *62–63*
    contemporary style, *10–11*
    drawings hung in, *130–131*
    lighting, *16*
    mix-and-match schemes, *12–13, 38–41*
    multipurpose, *14–15*
    "new classic," *32–33*

Living rooms *(contd.)*
    with personal style, *92–93*
    quilts hung in, *133*
    redecorating. *See* Changes, decorating
    shutters for window, *74*
    simplicity in, *28–29*
    staged decorating, *8–9, 118–121*
    starting-out scheme, *108-109*
    upholstery fabric, renewing with, *76–77*
Loft, *112–113*
Louis XVI chair, *150*
Love seats, *44, 77, 84–85, 92–93, 111*

M–P

Mail-order catalogs, 97
Mantel, *13*
Master bedrooms
    lighting, *17*
    starting-out scheme, *108*
    stripped-down look, *90–91*
    timelessness in, *30–31*
    wall coverings, judicious use of, *150*
Mies van der Rohe, Ludwig, 33
Minimalist approach to decorating, *26–27, 90–91*
Mini-slat blinds, 72, *73, 90*
    with old pieces, *30*
Modular coffee table, *120–121*
Modular seating pieces, *84–85, 108–109, 124–125*
Monochromatic scheme, *82–83*
Neutral schemes, *8–9*, 54
    with display items, *92–93*
    monochromatic, *82–83*
    plus one color, *80–81*
Office furniture, use of, 103
Oriental porcelain, *128*
Oriental rugs, *26–27, 38–41, 76–77*

Paint, use of, *116–117*
    architecture emphasized with, *88–89, 116–117*
    colors, *78–79*
Parsons table, *24–25*
Pastels, use of, in romantic decorating, *42–43*
Patterns
    in design collections, 100
    restraint in use of, *154–155*
Pencil-post bed, *30–31*
Pillow as sewing projects, *142–143*
    for child's room, 146, *147*
Pillow shams, floral, *86–87*
Platform beds, *42–43, 113*
Pleated balloon shade, *140*
Pleated draperies, 138, *139*
Pockets, storage, *146–147*
Porcelain, Oriental, *128*
Posters, *85, 106, 121*
Prints on walls, *32, 90–91, 121, 149*
Professional designers, use of, 20, 104

Q–T

Quilts, wall-hung, *133*
Rag rugs, *14–15, 23, 78–79, 117*
Recessed lighting, *16*
Rocking chair, twig, *149*
Rolled-arm seating pieces, *23*
Roman shades, *74–75, 141*
Romantic decorating, *42–45*
Round tablecloth, *145*
    making, *144*
Ruffled-edge pillow, *143*
Rugs
    dhurrie, *69, 84–85, 106–107, 115*
    geometric area rugs, *82–83*
    hooked, *24*
    Oriental, *26–27, 38–41, 76–77*
    rag, *14–15, 23, 78–79, 117*
    sisal, *111, 148–149*
Salvage firms, architectural, 103
School, converted to condominiums, *110*

Seating pieces
love seats, *44, 77, 84–85, 92–93, 111*
modular, *84–85, 108–109, 124–125*
in neutral-plus-one-color scheme, *80–81*
stools, *127*
upholstery fabric on, *22–23, 76–77*
wall color as background for, *78*
See also Chairs; Sofas
Settee, cane, *13*
Sewing projects, 138–147
children's accessories, *146–147*
curtains and draperies, *138–139*
pillows, *142–143*, 146, *147*
shades, *140–141*
table coverings, *144–145*
Shades, window, *74–75, 140–141*
Shelves
lights recessed beneath, *134–135*
around window, *92–93*
Shirred curtain, *138–139*
Shutters, *42–43*, 74
Sisal carpet, *70–71*
Sisal rugs, *111, 148–149*
Sitting room, *44–45*
Skylight, *67*
Sofas
contemporary, *8–9, 12–13*
fabric on, *76–77*
cotton, *70–71, 88–89*
for durability, *40–41*
flannel, *92–93*
re-covering job, *118–121*
velvet, *38–39*
white wool, *80–81*, 83
lighting in base, *136, 137*
L-shape, *21, 124–125*
off-white, *62–63*
Solarium, *114*
Sources of supply, 94–105
for antiques, 98, *99*
architectural salvage firms, 103
auctions, 98

Sources of supply *(contd.)*
catalogs, 97
department stores, 94
design collections, 100, *101*
display houses, 103
home stores, 94
import shops, 103
office supply stores, 103
professional designers, 104
specialty shops, 94
unfinished furniture, stores for, 103
Specialty shops, 94
Spiral staircase, *110–112*
Stenciled walls, *65*
Stools, *127*
Storage pockets, *146–147*
Style, *10–11*, 22–45
choosing, 48
handcrafted, *34–37*
mix-and-match, *12–13, 38–41*
romantic, *42–45*
simple, *26–29*
timeless, *30–33*
welcoming, *22–25*
Sun-porch-style kitchen, *6–7*
Table coverings, *144–145*
Tables, *23*
bamboo-base, *71*
Barcelona, *32–33*
carved and painted, *150–151*
coffee, *21*, 45
bench as, *59*
drum as, *78*
glass-topped, *9, 111*
mirror-finish, *88–89*
modular, *120–121*
Oriental-style, *83*
cubes, *109, 115*
dining
café table, *112*
as centerpiece of room, *26–27*
as desk, *114*
harvest-style, *122*

Tables *(contd.)*
marble-topped, *20–21*
parsons, 24–25
pine, *154*
skirted porch table as, *107*
in staged decorating, *118, 120*
drafting, *112–113, 123*
end table, wicker truck as, *108*
in kitchen, *34*
sofa table, *127*
Tie-backs, *72*, 138, *139*
Tile floors, *18–19, 66–67*, 69
Tizio lamps, *134, 136*
Track lighting, *17, 21, 32–33, 56–57*
Tract house, living/dining area in, *84–85*
Trellis designs, trompe l'oeil, *66, 150–151*
Trunk, wicker, *108*
Turkish corner pillows, 142–143, *143*

U–Z

Unfinished furniture, 103
Upholstered walls, *82–83*
Upholstery fabric, renewing with, *76–77*
Vinyl tiles, 69
Wall coverings, *64*, 65, *86–87*
on ceiling, *66*, 150
judicious use of, *150–151*
in patterned schemes, *154–155*
Wall treatments
and art display, 130
color for, *62–63*
with matching fabric, *86–87*
patterned, *64–65, 154–155*
restraint in, *150–151*
stenciled, *65*
upholstered, *82–83*
Wall unit/window seat, *108*
Wedding chairs, Scandinavian, *28, 29*
Wicker
chairs, *71, 125*
trunk, *108*

Windows
bay, *38–39*
treatments for, *74*
emphasizing, with paint, *88–89, 116–117*
shelves around, *92–93*
Window seat/wall unit, *108*
Window shades, *74–75, 140–141*
Window treatments, *72–75*, 80
floral fabric, *87*
draperies for French doors, *45*
light-admitting, 56
mini-slat blinds, *30*, 72, *73, 90*
sewing projects
curtains and draperies, *138–139*
shades, *140–141*
shutters, *42–43*, 74
Window walls, *18–19*
Windsor chair, *31*
Wing chairs, *9, 22–23*, 55
Wood ceiling, *66–67*
Wood floors, *68*, 69